THE BROTHERS GRIMM
Popular Folk Tales

THE
BROTHERS GRIMM
Popular Folk Tales

Newly Translated by Brian Alderson

Illustrated by Michael Foreman

DOUBLEDAY & COMPANY, INC.
GARDEN CITY, NEW YORK

ISBN 0 385 14356 7

Library of Congress Catalog Card Number 77–17748

Translation copyright © 1978 by Brian Alderson

Illustrations copyright © 1978 by Michael Foreman

This edition first published in 1978 by Victor Gollancz Limited, London

First Edition in the United States of America, 1978

Library of Congress Cataloging in Publication Data

Grimm, Jakob Ludwig Karl, 1785–1863.
    The Brothers Grimm popular folk tales.

    SUMMARY: Thirty-one folk and fairy tales collected by
the Grimm brothers including "Rapunzel," "Snow White," "The
Twelve Dancing Princesses," and "Hansel and Gretel."
        1. Fairy tales. (1. Fairy tales. 2. Folk-lore—Germany)
I. Grimm, Wilhelm Karl, 1786–1859, joint author.
II. Alderson, Brian W. III. Foreman, Michael, 1938–.
IV. Title. V. Title: Popular folk-tales.
PZ8.G882 By 1978   398.2
ISBN 0–385–14356–7

Printed in Great Britain by Westerham Press Ltd, Westerham, Kent

Contents

Contents (cont'd)

List of Colour Plates

THE BROTHERS GRIMM
Popular Folk Tales

Kinder- und Hausmärchen

Night gathers. Outside
All is comfortless:
Rain-dark, and the wide
Flat fields of weariness.

But here—at the fire—
Tom Cat, Curly-locks,
Old Aunt Maria
Wait for the story-box.

Then out come leaping
In raiment of words
Frog-princes, sleeping
Princesses, weeping
Sisters, and creeping
Witches, and cheeping,
Cackling, crying,
Singing, sighing,
Triumphantly flying
Magical birds.

$\mathcal{N}$ow, here's a story to begin with—

Not so long ago I saw a couple of roast chickens flying through the air. They flew very fast with their bellies towards Heaven and their backs towards Hell, while down below a millstone and an anvil were swimming across the river Rhine. (They swam very slowly and gracefully, and a frog sat on the ice beside them eating ploughshares at Whitsuntide.)

What's more there were three young fellows on crutches and stilts trying to catch a hare. The first was deaf, the second was blind, the third was dumb, and the fourth had lost the use of his legs. So do you want to know what happened? Well, the blind man caught sight of the hare trotting across the fields, and the dumb man called out to the lame man with the news, and the lame man caught the hare by its collar. There were some others too, who wanted to sail on the land, so they spread their sails to the wind and took ship over the meadows: and they sailed and sailed till they got to a high mountain where, I'm sorry to say, they all drowned. Meanwhile a crab had joined in the hunt for the hare and a cow was lying on top of the roof where she'd climbed up to look for grass.

> *In that land the flies*
> *Are big as cabbage-pies.*
> *Now open up the window*
> *And let out all the lies.*

Little Louse and Little Flea

A little louse and a little flea kept house together and brewed their beer in an egg-shell. But the little louse fell in and burned himself up. So straight away the little flea began a wild crying and lamenting and the little door of her room said, "Little Flea, why do you weep?"

"Because Little Louse has burnt himself up."

So then the little door began to creak, and a little broom in the corner said, "Little Door, why do you creak?"

"Why shouldn't I creak?
Little Louse has burnt himself up, and
Little Flea weeps."

Then the little broom began sweeping like mad, and a little truck came trundling by and said, "Little Broom, why do you sweep?"

"Why shouldn't I sweep?
Little Louse has burnt himself up,
Little Flea weeps, and
Little Door creaks."

Then the little truck said, "So I will run," and he began to run, squeaking like mad. And he ran squeaking past the muck-heap, who said, "Little Truck, why do you squeak?"

"Why shouldn't I squeak?
Little Louse has burnt himself up,
Little Flea weeps,
Little Door creaks, and
Little Broom sweeps."

Then the little muck-heap said, "So I will burn like mad," and he began to shoot out smoke and flames. And there was a little tree standing by the little muck-heap, and he said, "Little Muck- Heap, why do you smoke?"

"Why shouldn't I smoke?
Little Louse has burnt himself up,
Little Flea weeps,
Little Door creaks,
Little Broom sweeps, and
Little Truck squeaks."

Then the little tree said, "So I will shake myself," and he began to shake so that all his leaves fell off. A little girl, passing by with a little water-jug, saw all that and said, "Little Tree, why do you shake yourself?"

"Why shouldn't I shake myself?
Little Louse has burnt himself up,
Little Flea weeps,
Little Door creaks,
Little Broom sweeps,
Little Truck squeaks, and
The Muck-Heap smokes."

Then the little girl said, "So I will break my jug," and she broke her little water-jug. Then the little spring from which the water rose said, "Little Girl, why do you break your little water-jug?"

"Why shouldn't I break my little water-jug?
Little Louse has burnt himself up,
Little Flea weeps,
Little Door creaks,
Little Broom sweeps
Little Truck squeaks,
The Muck-Heap smokes, and
The Little Tree shakes."

"Hayday!" said the little spring. "So I'll begin to flood." And he began to flood like mad and everyone was drowned in the water: the little girl, the little tree, the little muck-heap, the little truck, the little broom, the little door, the little flea and the little louse. They were all drowned together.

Whisp of Straw, Lump of Coal, and Little Broad Bean

In a village not far from here there lived a poor old woman who'd got herself a dish of beans and was going to boil them up for her supper. So she made up a fire in the hearth and to hasten it along she used a handful of straw to light it. But when she tipped the beans into the pot one of them fell on the floor without her noticing and came to rest by a bit of the straw. Soon afterwards a glowing lump of coal jumped from the fire down beside the other two.

The whisp of straw opened up a conversation. "Well now, friends," he said, "where have you come from?"

And the lump of coal answered, "With the greatest of good fortune I've jumped out of that fire. If I hadn't managed to do it I was bound for certain death—I'd have been burnt to ashes."

And the bean said," Yes, me too. I've only just been able to save my skin. If the old woman had tipped me into that pot I'd have been boiled up into mash like all my friends."

"And would I have had any better fate?" asked the straw. "That old woman has sent my brothers up in smoke and flames. Sixty of 'em jampacked to the slaughter, but luckily for me I slipped through her fingers."

"Well what are we going to do with ourselves?" asked the lump of coal.

"I think," said the bean, "that since we've all been lucky enough to escape a nasty death we should become good companions; and for fear of any more disasters overtaking us here we should go on the road together and leave straightway for another country."

The other two were pleased with this suggestion and so they all set out. It wasn't long, though, before they came to a little stream, and since there was no bridge or plank across it they had no idea how they were to get to the other side. But the straw was struck with a good idea and said, "Look here; I'll lie down across the stream and you two can use me as a bridge." And the straw lay down, stretching himself from one bank to the other, and the lump of coal (who had an impulsive nature) immediately began to scamper over this newly opened bridge. But when he got to the middle and heard the water rushing below him he took fright, stood stock-still and wouldn't trust himself to move an inch further. This caused the straw to catch alight and it broke into two pieces and fell into the stream. The lump of coal tumbled in after, sizzled as it hit the water and then gave up the ghost.

The bean, who had prudently stayed on the bank all this time, couldn't help laughing when he saw what happened. In fact he just couldn't stop, and he laughed so hard that he burst. And that, I'm afraid would have been the end of him except that, to his great good fortune, a travelling tailor was having a rest down there beside the stream. And since this tailor was a kind-hearted fellow he fetched out his needle and thread and sewed the bean together again. The bean thanked him with a great show of gratitude, but because the tailor had sewn him up with black thread, beans from his family have always had a black seam down the middle from that day to this.

The Bremen Town Musicians

A man had a donkey and for years this donkey carried the man's sacks to the mill without any grumbling. But now he was coming to the end of his strength so that day by day he got less and less capable. Then his master decided to do away with him; but the donkey saw which way the wind was blowing and took himself off, setting out down the road to Bremen. "There," says he to himself, "I can surely get a job as a town musician."

Well, after he'd gone along for a bit he came on a hunting-dog lying in the road panting like someone who's run himself to a standstill. "Now then, Caesar," says he, "what are you puffing and blowing like that for?"

"Ah!" says the dog. "Just because I'm old and getting weaker every day, just because I can't go hunting any more, my master wants to kill me. So I've taken myself off—but where I'm going to get a living I'm sure I don't know."

"I'll tell you what," says the donkey, "I'm going to Bremen to be a town musician. Why don't you come with me and the two of us can take up music together. I'll play the lute and you can bang the drum." Well, the dog was pleased about that and the two of them went on down the road.

They hadn't gone far when they came on a cat sitting in the middle of the road with a face like a week of wet Mondays. "Now what's upsetting you, old Whisker-wiper?" says the donkey.

"Ah!" says the cat, "what's so jolly about having your neck wrung? Just because I'm getting on a bit and my teeth aren't so sharp as they used to be and I prefer to sit by the fire and purr rather than chase around after mice, my old woman wants to drown me. True, I've got away this far, but now it's hard to come by good advice and I don't know where to go next."

"Well—you must come with us to Bremen. You're a good chap for serenading, you can be a town musician along with us." The cat thought that was a good idea and joined them.

Soon after this the three travellers passed a farmyard, and there, sitting on the gate, was a cock, crowing away for dear life. "You're making enough noise to freeze a man's bones," said the donkey, "what's the matter with you?"

"Here have I been calling up good weather for Saturday," said the cock, "but just because tomorrow's Sunday and we've got company coming, the old farmer's wife's not having any mercy. She's told the cook she wants to have me in tomorrow's soup, and this evening they're going to chop my head off. So I'm using up my voice while I still can."

"Hey, then, old Redpoll," said the donkey, "why don't you come along with us? We're going to Bremen, and, whatever happens, you're sure to find something better there than a stew-pot. You've certainly got a good voice, and if we all make music in a group it's bound to have a bit of class." Naturally the idea pleased the cock and all four of them went on their way together.

But Bremen wasn't to be reached in a day, and by evening they'd come to a wood where they decided to spend the night. The donkey and the dog lay down to sleep under a large tree, and the cat and the cock climbed up into the branches—the cock flying right up to the crown of the tree where he'd be safest. Before he fell asleep he looked around him for a last time in all directions, and it seemed to him he could see a little glimmer of light glowing in the distance. So he called down to his friends that there must be a house not so far away because a lamp was shining. So the donkey said, "Very well, let's all get up again and go on a bit further. The lodging's pretty awful here for sure," and the dog remarked that a couple of bones and a chunk of meat would do him a world of good. So they set off again in the direction of the light, and soon they saw that it was getting brighter, and it grew bigger and bigger, till they finally came to a brightly lit robbers' house.

Since he was the biggest, the donkey went up to the window and looked inside. "What's to be seen, old Greycoat?" asked the cock.

"What's to be seen?" said the donkey, "why, there's a table set there with lots of fancy stuff to eat and drink, and robbers sitting round it enjoying themselves."

"That looks like something for us," said the cock.

"Right you are," said the donkey, "I wish we were there."

Then the animals put their heads together to decide what they might do to chase out the robbers, and at last they hit on a plan. The donkey was to stand with his front hooves against the window, the dog was to jump on the donkey's back, the cat was to climb on the dog, and, last of all, the cock was to fly up and sit up there on the cat's head. When that was done they waited for a signal and then, all together, they struck up a tune. The donkey yelled, the dog barked, the cat miaowed, and the cock crew. Then they all fell into the room through the window with glass crashing all around them. The robbers leapt up at such a terrible din, thinking they were being attacked by boggarts, and they rushed off into the wood in a panic. So our four friends sat themselves down round the table, picked out what they liked best from everything left there, and ate enough to last them the next three weeks.

When the four minstrels were finished they put out the light and looked for somewhere to sleep, each one to his own taste. The donkey lay down on the dung-heap, the dog behind the door, the cat on the hearth by the warm ashes, and the cock up on the roof-tree; and because they were tired after their long journey, they fell asleep at once.

When midnight was past and the robbers saw from a distance that no lights were burning in the house any more and that everything seemed peaceful, their captain said, "We shouldn't have let ourselves be pushed about like that"—and he ordered one of his men back to the house to see what was going on.

The one who'd been sent found everything quiet. He went into the kitchen to strike a light and because he mistook the glowing fiery eyes of the cat for live coals he held a match to them to get it lit. But the cat didn't think much of that for a game and sprang at his face, spitting and scratching. This gave him a nasty fright and he ran off to try to get out by the back door. But the dog, who was lying there, bit him in the leg, and as he ran across the yard by the dung-heap, the donkey gave him a smart kick with one of his hind legs. As for the cock, though—woken out of his slumbers by all this racket—he cheered up no end and shouted out from the roof-tree, "Cack-a-doodle-doo! Cack-a-doodle-doo!"

Then the robber ran as best he could back to his captain and said, "Aaah! There's a fearful witch sitting in that house and she's spat at me and scratched my face with her nails. And by the door there's a man with a knife, who stuck me in the leg; and in the yard there's a black monster who let fly at me with a wooden club. And up there on the roof there's a judge sitting, calling out, 'Hang him in a noose. Hang him in a noose!' So I got out as quick as I could."

And from that time on the robbers wouldn't trust themselves to go near the house. But as for the four Bremen Town Musicians, it suited them so well that they never wanted to leave it to go on with their journey.

So that's the story, and the last one who told it got a plateful of muffins for his pains.

Enter three musicians on their way to Bremen

The Wolf and the Seven Little Kids

Once upon a time there was a nanny-goat who had seven young kids. Well one day she had to go out and she told them that, whatever they did, they must watch out for the wolf and be sure never to let him into the house.

Soon after this the wolf came up to the goats' little house and said, "Children, dear children, please let me in; I am your mother come back home again."

But the seven little kids said, "Our mother hasn't got a croaky voice like that; you're the wolf, you're never our mother."

So the wolf had to go away; and he went to the grocer's and bought some chalk, which he ate to make his voice all soft. Then he went back to the cottage and called out cheerily, "Children, dear children, please let your mother in."

But he'd stretched out his paws on the window-sill and the little kids said, "Our mother hasn't got black feet like that, so you certainly can't come in because you're the wolf."

So now the wolf took himself off to the baker's and said, "Baker, cover my paws with nice fresh dough." And when that was done he went to the miller's and said, "Miller, cover my paws with nice fresh flour." But the miller would do no such thing, so the wolf threatened to eat him up, body and bones, and the miller *had* to do it.

When the wolf came back to the house and asked to be let in the seven little kids once more demanded to see his feet, but when he held them up to the window and they saw that the paws were all white they believed that it truly was their mother come home again, and they ran to open the door.

As soon as they realised that it was still the wolf they dashed about in a panic and hid themselves as best they could: one under the table, another in the bed, the third in the stove, the fourth in the kitchen, the fifth in the cupboard, the sixth under a great big soup-tureen and the seventh in the grandfather clock. In spite of all this, though, the wolf found every one of them and swallowed them down with relish—except for the youngest in the clock. Then he took himself off, and when the mother-goat returned it was left to this youngest little kid to jump out of his hiding-place and tell her everything that had happened.

Now the wolf, because he was full up, went away to a nice green meadow, settled himself down in the sunshine and fell straight into a deep sleep. So when she saw this, the nanny-goat called to her youngest child to fetch scissors, needle, and thread and they cut open the wolf's fat belly and out jumped the six little brothers and sisters, all unharmed, because the wolf had swallowed them whole. Then they fetched a lot of big round stones, put them all inside the wolf, and sewed him up again with needle and thread.

When the wolf had had his sleep, he woke up and felt this great weight in his belly and he said to himself, "Well I don't know! What's all this rumbling and tumbling inside my tum? What's all this rumbling and tumbling inside my tum? After all, I've only had six little kids to eat, and they're not much." So he set off for a nearby well to get himself a drink, but when he got there the weight of the stones in his belly toppled him over into the water. And when the seven little kids saw that, they came up, joined hands in a circle, and danced ring o'roses round the well.

The Seven Ravens

There was a man had seven sons, but never a little daughter, much as he wanted one. At last, though, his wife gave sign of some happy expectations, and when the child came into the world it was indeed a little girl. Joy enough at that—true—but the child was small and puny, and everyone thought need of a speedy christening on account of her delicacy. So the father sent one of the boys off to the well, quick, to fetch some christening-water, and the other six went with him. But because they all wanted to be first to bring up the water the jug fell into the well.

So—they all stood round and couldn't think what to do, for not one of them dared to go back home. And when they didn't arrive the old father lost all patience and said, "To be sure, they've gone off on some prank or other and forgotten all about us, the little devils."

He was frantic the little girl would die without being christened and in his consternation he cried out, "Would that those lads were all turned into ravens," and hardly were the words spoken than he heard a whirring sound in the sky over his head. He looked up and saw seven coal-black ravens flying away.

The stars point the way to the seven ravens

No chance now of the parents ever taking back such a curse—but for all their sadness over the loss of their seven sons, at least they could comfort themselves a bit over their darling daughter, who soon picked up in strength, and grew more beautiful every day that passed. For a long time though, she knew nothing about having all those brothers, because her parents took good care not to mention the fact, till one day she chanced to hear some folks saying: True, the girl was beautiful enough, but no doubt at all that she was guilty of her seven brothers' misfortune.

She was altogether cast down by this, went to her father and mother and asked them: What about these brothers then and where'd they gone to? So the parents couldn't keep things hushed up any more and said it was a judgement of Heaven and her birth had been the innocent cause of all the trouble. But day-by-day the girl felt the matter more and more deeply and brought herself to the idea that she must go to release her brothers. She couldn't sleep; she couldn't rest; and at last she got up all unbeknown to the others and set off into the wide world to find where her brothers were and to set them free, no matter what the cost. She took nothing with her, save a little ring, as a reminder of her parents, a loaf of bread, against hunger, a little jug of water, against thirst, and a little stool, against weariness.

So she walked, and she walked, and she walked, far off to the very end of the world. There she came to the Sun, but he was too hot and fearsome, and gobbled up little children. She ran away from him quick, and ran to the Moon, but he was altogether too cold. He was nasty and evil too and when he saw the child he said, "I smell the smell of human flesh." So she made off as fast as she could and came to the Stars, who were friendly and kind to her—each one sitting on his own special stool. As for the Star of Morning though, he stood up, gave her a little leg of a chicken and said, "Without this chicken's leg you cannot open the Glass Mountain, and in the Glass Mountain there you will find your brothers."

The girl took the little chicken leg, wrapped it up carefully in her handkerchief, and then walked and walked and walked till she came to the Glass Mountain. The gate there was shut tight and she needed the chicken leg for it, but when she undid her handkerchief it was empty. She'd lost the gift of the kindly Stars.

What to do now? She was determined to rescue her brothers but had no key to the gate of the Glass Mountain. So this brave little sister took a knife, cut off one of her own little fingers, poked it into the lock and let the gate triumphantly swing wide. When she'd got in, a little dwarf came up to her and said, "My child, what are you looking for?"

"I'm looking for my brothers, the seven ravens," she answered.

Then the dwarf said, "My Lords the Ravens are not at home, but if you would wait here until their return, then come in"—and the little dwarf brought in the seven ravens' food and drink on seven little plates and in seven little mugs, and from each little plate the sister took a little crumb and from each little mug she drank a little sip; but in the last mug of all she let fall the little ring that she had brought with her.

Suddenly there was a whirring noise in the air and the sound of cawing. "Now my Lords the Ravens come flying home," said the little dwarf. And they came, and would eat and drink, and sought their little plates and their little mugs.

Then, one after another, they said, "Who's been eating from my little plate? Who's been drinking from my little mug? Here is the taste of human lips," and when the seventh raven drained his little mug dry, out rolled the ring.

He looked at it, and knew it for the ring that belonged to his father and mother, and he said, "Would to God that our sister were here, then were we free." Well, the girl was standing behind the door, listening, and when she heard him wish that wish she stepped forward and straight away the ravens took on their human form again. And they hugged and kissed one another and set off gaily home.

Rapunzel

Once upon a time there was a man and his wife and they longed and longed to have a child—but all in vain. Then, at last, the woman began to hope that the good Lord might indeed grant their wishes.

Now these people had a little window at the back of their house, and through it you could see into a marvellous garden, all full of the most beautiful plants and flowers. But this garden was set about with a great high wall and nobody dared to go in because it belonged to a sorceress who was possessed of great powers and was feared by everyone.

One day the woman stood at this little window and looked down into the garden, where she happened to see a flower-bed given over to the most beautiful rapunzel-plants, and they seemed so fresh and green that her mouth watered and she was filled with a great desire to eat them. And this desire grew fiercer day by day and since she knew that there was no way for her to come by the rapunzels she fell into a decline, turning pale and miserable.

Well her husband was frightened by this and asked her what it was she was pining for; and she answered, "Ah—if I don't get any of those rapunzels growing in the garden out the back then I shall die."

So the man, who loved her very much, said to himself, "Hey then,

better to fetch rapunzels than let your wife go to her grave—and hang
the cost"—and in the evening twilight he climbed up over the wall into
the garden of the sorceress, grabbed a handful of rapunzel-plants as
quick as he could and brought them to his wife. Straight away she made
up a rapunzel-salad for herself and swallowed it down with great gulps.

This salad had tasted so very, very good that the next day her longing
was three times as great—if she was ever to be at peace, then her man
must once again climb over into the garden. So once more he went down
in the evening twilight, but when he'd climbed down from the wall he
was terrified to find the sorceress standing in front of him.

"How can you dare," she said—her eyes flashing with rage—"to
climb into my garden like a common thief and steal my rapunzels? This
shall be the worse for you."

"Aiee," he answered, "you're right—what you say is true—but
please have mercy. I've been driven to what I've done because I needed
to: my wife saw your rapunzels out of the window, and felt so great a
longing for them that she would have died if she hadn't had some to
eat."

Then the sorceress cooled her anger and said to him, "Very well, if
things are as you say they are, then I shall let you take away as many
rapunzel-plants as you wish; but I make one condition. You must give
me the child that your wife will bring into the world. All will go well with
it. I shall care for it like a mother."

In his anguish the man agreed to everything, and when the woman's
baby was born the sorceress immediately appeared, named the child
"Rapunzel" and took it away with her.

Rapunzel was the most beautiful child in all the world. When she was
twelve years old, the sorceress shut her up in a tower that lay deep in a
forest and had neither door nor stairway, but only a little window at the
top. And whenever the sorceress wanted to come in she would stand
below and call out:

> "Rapunzel, Rapunzel,
>   Let down your hair to me,"

for Rapunzel had long, beautiful hair, as fine as spun gold. And when
she heard the voice of the sorceress she would loosen her tresses, wrap
them round a window-hook and then let her hair fall to the ground

twenty yards below and the sorceress would climb up it.

Now it so happened that after a couple of years a king's son was riding through the forest and came past the tower. There he heard a song that was so lovely that he stood stock-still and listened. It was Rapunzel, who in her loneliness, passed her time singing, with the sweetest voice you ever heard. The prince wanted to go up to her and looked for a door to the tower, but none was to be found, so he rode home. But his heart had been so touched by the song, that he went out to the wood every day and listened. Then, once, as he stood behind a tree, he saw that a sorceress came by and he heard how she called out:

"Rapunzel, Rapunzel,
Let down your hair."

Then Rapunzel let down her tresses and the sorceress climbed up to her. "Well, if that's the ladder that you have to climb," said the prince to himself, "then I'll try my luck too," and the next day, when it began to get dark, he went to the tower and called out:

"Rapunzel, Rapunzel,
Let down your hair,"

and straight away the hair came tumbling down and the king's son made his way up.

To begin with Rapunzel was terribly afraid to see a man come in through the window, for she'd never seen such a thing before; but the young prince began to talk to her, very friendly, and told her that her singing so touched his heart that it gave him no peace and he had to see the singer herself. So Rapunzel lost her fear, and when he asked her if she would have him for her husband, and she saw that he was young and handsome, she thought to herself, "He'll be kinder to me than that old godmother"—so she said yes and laid her hand in his hand.

Then she said, "I would like to go with you, but I don't know how I can get down. Every time you come to see me, bring a thread of silk and I will weave a ladder from them, and when it's ready then I'll climb down and you can carry me away on your horse."

They agreed that, till then, he should come to her every evening, since the old woman came to her in the day-time, and the sorceress noticed nothing of this till one day Rapunzel said to her, "Tell me, little Godmother, why is it that you're so much more of a weight climbing up

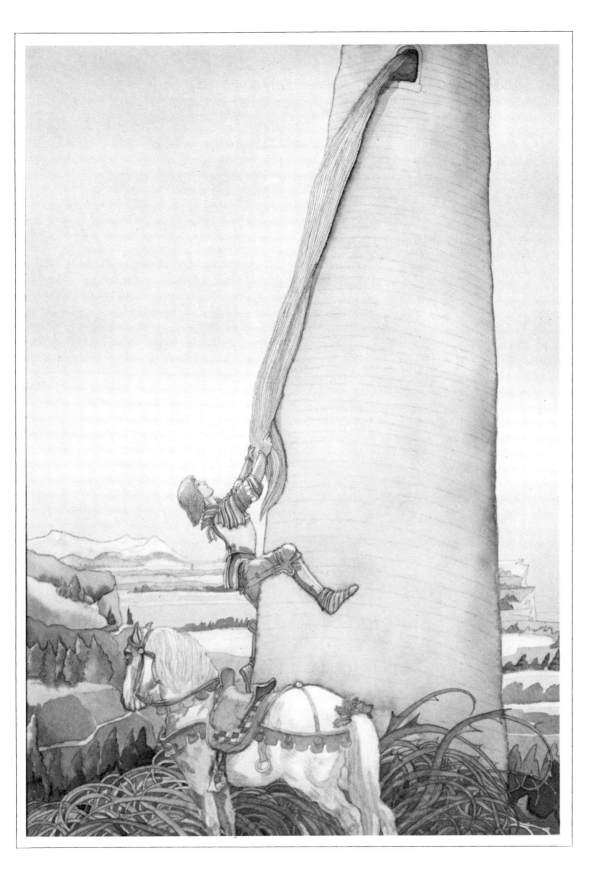

than that young prince? He's up here in a moment."

"Aaah! you godless creature," cried the sorceress. "What's this I hear you say? Here am I, thinking I've parted you from all the world and you've betrayed me!" And in her anger she grasped Rapunzel's beautiful hair, twisted it round her left hand a couple of times, seized the scissors with her right and—ritch, ratch—it was all cut off and the lovely tresses lay on the ground. And so unmerciful was she that, by her powers, she brought Rapunzel into a waste-land where she had to live in sorrow and misery.

In the evening of the selfsame day that she had cast out Rapunzel, the sorceress fastened the shorn hair to the window-hook and when the prince came and called out:

"Rapunzel, Rapunzel,
Let down your hair,"

she let down the hair. The prince climbed up, but when he got to the top he found, not his dearest Rapunzel, but the sorceress who regarded him with looks of poisonous evil. "Aha!" she mocked, "you're after fetching Darling Madam are you? Well the pretty bird isn't sitting on the nest any more, isn't singing any more. The cat's got her—and will have your eyes out too! Rapunzel's lost to you and you won't see her again."

The prince went out of his mind with grief, and in his despair he jumped down from the tower. He got away with his life but the thorn bushes that he fell into scratched out both his eyes. And so he wandered blindly through the forest, eating nothing but roots and berries, and doing nothing but weep and lament over the loss of his darling wife. In this way he roved in misery for some years until eventually he came to the waste-land where Rapunzel lived in great distress, with a pair of twins who had been born to her—a little boy and a little girl. The prince heard her voice, and it sounded so familiar to him that he made towards it, and when he came up to her Rapunzel recognised him, put her arms round his neck and wept.

It so happened though, that two of her tears fell upon his eyes, and they became clear again and he could see as well as ever before. So he carried Rapunzel into his own kingdom, where he was received with great joy, and the two of them lived happily ever after.

travelling through the land. An old man told him how people believed that a castle stood behind the hedge of thorns with a beautiful princess sleeping there and all her court. He said his grandfather had told him how many a prince had come in times past, seeking to force a way through, but how they'd all been caught up in the thorns and pricked to death.

"That's not something to scare me," said the king's son. "I'll get through the hedge and set the beautiful Briar-Rose free," and he went off.

When he came to the hedge of thorns it changed to blossoming flowers, which parted to let him through, and turned to thorns behind him again. Then he came to the castle, and in the courtyard the horses lay sleeping, and the brindled hunting-dogs, and on the roof the pigeons sat with their heads tucked under their wings. And, when he entered the building, the flies were sleeping on the wall, and the fire in the kitchen-hearth, and the cook still held up his hand to clout the kitchen-boy, and the maid still had the old black hen in front of her. So he went further, and there lay the royal court sleeping, and further still, there were the king and queen—and everything was so quiet that he could hear himself breathing.

At last he came to the old tower and there, at the top, lay the Princess Briar-Rose, sleeping. And the king's son was so amazed at her beauty that he bent down and kissed her, and in that moment she awoke. Then too the king and queen awoke and their courtiers, looking at each other in astonishment, and the horses shook themselves, and the dogs jumped about and wagged their tails, and the pigeons on the roof took their heads out from under their wings, looked around, and flew off to the fields, and the flies on the wall began to crawl again, and the fire sprang up and flared and finished cooking the dinner; the roast went on spitting and the cook boxed the kitchen-boy's ears and the maid plucked all the feathers from the hen.

Then the marriage was celebrated between Briar-Rose and the king's son and they lived happily to the end of their days.

Jorinde and Joringel

Once upon a time in the middle of a huge dark forest there stood an ancient castle, and in this castle there lived an old, ancient woman—all alone, for she was a witch. In the day-time she would turn herself into a cat or into a screech-owl, but at night she took the form of an ordinary mortal again. She had the power to tempt wild animals and birds to come to her, and then she would kill them and boil them up in a stew. And if any other human-being came within a hundred paces of her castle, then he would find himself frozen fast, not able to shift from the spot till she unspelled him, but if it was an innocent young girl who came into the circle then she would turn her into a bird and shut her up in a wicker-work cage and carry the cage to one of the chambers of the castle. Altogether she had seven thousand such cages in the castle, all full of the rarest birds.

Now you ought to know that there was once a young girl who was called Jorinde—more beautiful than any other girl you can think of; and she and a boy called Joringel, who was just as handsome, were pledged to be married. They were in the days leading up to the wedding and they had eyes only for each other, and one time—in order to get away and talk to each other alone— they went to walk in the forest.

"Be careful," said Joringel, "that you don't come too near the castle." Ah! but what a beautiful evening it was! The sun shone between the trunks of the trees, bringing radiance to the green depths of the forest, and a turtle-dove sang dolefully among the ancient hawthorns.

Jorinde wept from time to time—sat herself down in the sunshine and sorrowed; and Joringel sorrowed too. They were cast down, as though the time had come for them to die. They looked about themselves, took the wrong path, and lost all sense of how they might get home again. The sun still stood half above the mountain, but half was already behind. Joringel looked through the bushes and saw, all too close to them, the old walls of the castle; he started and was filled with terror. Jorinde just sang:

> "My little bird with ring so red
>   Sings sorrow, sorrow, sorrow
>   He sings to the little dove that he is dead
>   Sings sorrow, sorr-oochickee, chickoo, chickee."

Joringel looked at Jorinde. Jorinde was transformed into a nightingale, singing "chickoo, chickoo". A screech-owl, with burning eyes, flew three times round her, three times crying "Hoo, hoo, hoo"; and Joringel could not move. He stood there like a stone—could neither weep nor speak, could move neither hand nor foot.

Now the sun was down. The owl flew into a bush, and straight away a bent old woman stepped out, skinny and yellow, with big red eyes and a hooky nose whose point reached down to her chin. She muttered something, caught up the nightingale and carried it away on her hand. Joringel could say nothing, could not move from the spot. The nightingale was gone.

Eventually the old woman came back again and said in a hollow voice, "Greetings, Zakiel. When moon shines in cage, unloose, Zakiel. The hour is come." And Joringel was free. He fell on his knees before the old woman and begged her to give him back his Jorinde again, but she said he should never have her more, and went away. He shouted, he

Joringel trapped

wept, he yammered, but all in vain. "Ooooh—what shall become of me!"

Joringel went away and came at last to a village where nobody knew him, and there for a long time he looked after the sheep. He would often go and walk round the castle—but never too near. Then, eventually, one night he dreamed that he found a blood-red flower, and in the middle of the flower was a large, beautiful pearl. He broke the flower from its stalk and went with it to the castle; and everything that he touched with the flower was freed from enchantment. He dreamed, too, that in this way he gained his Jorinde again.

Next morning, when he awoke, he set out across mountains and valleys to see if he could discover such a flower. For nine days he sought it, and then, early one morning, he found the blood-red flower and in its centre was a huge drop of dew, as large as the most beautiful pearl. Travelling by night and day he brought this flower to the castle. When he came within a hundred paces of the castle walls, he wasn't held fast but went on up to the great gateway.

Joringel rejoiced. He touched the gate with the flower and it sprang open. He went in, through the courtyard, and listened for the sound of all the birds. At last he heard it. He went and found the chamber, and there was the witch, feeding the birds in their seven thousand cages. When she saw Joringel she turned on him in fury, wicked fury. She cursed him, spat gall and poison at him, but she couldn't move two steps towards him. For his part he didn't heed her and went looking at the cages and the birds; but there were hundreds upon hundreds of nightingales, how should he discover which one was his Jorinde?

While he was searching like this he noticed that the old woman was creeping away with one bird in a little cage, carrying it towards the door. Straightway he leapt across the room, touched the little cage with the flower and the old woman too. From that moment her magic powers fled away, and Jorinde stood before him and kissed him, as beautiful as ever she'd been before. Then he turned all the other birds back into young girls again, and he and his Jorinde returned home and lived happily ever after.

Little Brother and Little Sister

Little Brother took Little Sister by the hand and said, "We've not had a moment's happiness since our mother died. Our stepmother beats us every day, and kicks us every time we come near her. All we get to eat are the leftover crusts, and even the dog does better than that under the table—she's forever tossing stuff down there for him. Pray God, our true mother doesn't know what's happening! So come on—let's see what we can find for ourselves out there in the wide world."

For a whole day they walked over meadows and fields and stony places, and whenever it rained Little Sister said, "God and our hearts are crying together!" And in the evening they came to a great forest and, what with sadness and hunger and the long journey, they were so tired that they settled down in a hollow tree and went to sleep.

The next morning, when they woke up, the sun was already high in the sky and was shining brightly into their tree. Then Little Brother said, "I'm thirsty, Little Sister. If I knew of a spring I'd go and get a drink. Listen! I think I can hear one running." Little Brother stood up and took Little Sister by the hand and they set out to look for the brook.

47

But their wicked stepmother was a witch and she'd seen well enough how the children had gone off together and she'd crept after them, secretly, as witches creep, and had put a spell on all the streams of the forest. So now, when they found a little spring, bubbling up over the stones, all silvery, Little Brother knelt down to drink. But Little Sister heard what it said as it flowed by:

"Whoever drinks of me will turn into a tiger; whoever drinks of me will turn into a tiger," and Little Sister cried out, "Please, Little Brother, please don't drink it, otherwise you'll turn into a wild beast and tear me to pieces." So Little Brother didn't drink although he was so thirsty and he said, "I'll wait till we get to the next spring." When they came to this second brooklet, Little Sister heard how it said:

"Whoever drinks of me will turn into a wolf; whoever drinks of me will turn into a wolf," and Little Sister cried out, "Please, Little Brother, please, don't drink it, otherwise you'll turn into a wolf and eat me up." So Little Brother didn't drink, but said, "Very well, I'll wait till we come to the next spring, but then I *must* drink, whatever you say, because I'm so thirsty." And when they came to the third brooklet Little Sister heard what it said as it flowed by:

"Whoever drinks of me will turn into a deer; whoever drinks of me will turn into a deer." Then Little Sister said, "Ah, Little Brother, please, please, don't drink, otherwise you'll turn into a deer and run away from me." But Little Brother had already knelt down by the stream, bent over and drunk the water, and as the first drops touched his lips, he lay there, a little fawn.

Little Sister wept for her poor, bewitched brother, and the little fawn wept too, sitting sadly beside her. Then at last the little girl said, "Quiet, quiet, Little Fawn. I won't ever, ever, leave you." And she untied her golden garter and put it round the little fawn's neck, and she picked rushes and plaited them into a soft rope as a lead for the creature—then she led him on, deeper and deeper into the forest. And after they had gone on a long, long time they came at last to a little house and the young girl looked inside and, because it was empty, she thought, "Here we can stay and live."

So she looked for leaves and moss to make a soft couch for the little

Little Brother drinks at the third stream

fawn, and every morning she went out and gathered roots and berries and nuts, and brought back fresh grass for the creature, who ate it out of her hand, was content and played happily in front of her. And every evening when Little Sister was tired and had said her prayers she would lay her head on Little Fawn's back, and he was like a soft pillow for her to sleep on. If only Little Brother had had his human form it would have been a wonderful life.

This lonely existence in the wilds went on for some time. Then, one day, it so happened that the king of that country led a great hunt into the forest. There was a mighty blowing of horns, barking of dogs, and yelling of huntsmen among the trees, and Little Fawn heard it and longed to be there too.

"Oh," he said to Little Sister, "let me go out to the hunt, I can't bear to be here any longer," and he pleaded with her so long that she finally agreed.

"But be sure to come back to me by evening," she said to him, "because I shall bolt the door against wild beasts. And so that I'll know it's you, knock on the door and say 'Sisterling, let me in'—and if you don't say that I won't open the door."

So the little fawn ran off, bounding and rejoicing in the open air. Before long the king and his huntsmen saw the beautiful creature and set out after him, but they couldn't catch up with him, and when they thought that they had him for sure then he'd leap away over the underwoods and disappear. Then, when it got dark he ran back to the little house, knocked, and said, "Sisterling, let me in," and the little door was opened for him and he leapt inside and rested the whole night on his soft couch.

The next morning the hunt was up again, and when Little Fawn heard the blowing of the horns and the "Ho, ho" of the hunters he could not rest, and he said, "Little Sister, open the door for me, I must be out and away." So Little Sister opened the door for him, saying, "But remember, you must come back here this evening and say your rhyme."

When the king and his huntsmen once again saw the little fawn with his golden collar they all chased after him, but he was too nimble and quick for them. The hunt lasted the whole day until, at last, in the evening, the hunters had surrounded him and one of them wounded him in the foot so that he had to limp and could only escape with great difficulty. Then one of the huntsmen trailed him back to the little house and heard how he called "Sisterling, let me in," and saw how the door was opened for him and just as quickly closed again. The huntsman made sure that he could remember everything that had happened, went back to the king and told him all that he'd seen and heard. And the king said, "Tomorrow we shall hunt once more."

As for Little Sister, she was terribly frightened when she saw that Little Fawn was wounded. She cleaned away the blood, dressed the wound with herbs, and said, "Off to bed with you, my dearest Little Fawn, so that you'll get better again." But the wound was such a tiny one that, by morning, Little Fawn couldn't feel it at all. And when he heard the racket of the hunt going on again outside, he said, "I can't bear it—I must be there. Don't worry, no one will catch me."

But Little Sister cried and said, "Now they'll kill you for sure, and I shall be left alone in the forest, lost to the world. I shan't let you go."

"Then I'll stay here and die of melancholy," answered Little Fawn. "When I hear those hunting-horns I think I could jump out of my very shoes."

So there was nothing for it but Little Sister must, with a heavy heart, open the door for him, and the little fawn ran off, well and cheerful, into the forest. When the king spotted him, he said to his huntsmen, "Now, hunt him down the whole day until nightfall, but let no one harm him." And as soon as the sun had set the king said to the huntsman, "Now, come and show me the little house in the woods." And when he stood before the little door he knocked and called, "Dear Sisterling, let me in." Then the door was opened and the king walked in, and there stood a young girl more beautiful than any he had ever seen before.

The girl was terrified when she saw that it wasn't her little fawn that she'd let in, but a man with a golden crown on his head, but the king looked at her kindly, held out his hand to her, and said, "Will you come with me, back to my castle, and will you be my wife?"

"Ah, yes," answered the girl, "but Little Fawn must come too. I'll never leave him."

And the king said, "He shall stay by you as long as you live and shall want for nothing."

Meanwhile Little Fawn had come running home, and Little Sister put on his lead of plaited rushes again, took it in her own hand and went with him away from the little house in the woods.

The king took the beautiful young girl up on his own horse and brought her to his castle where their marriage was celebrated with great splendour. So now she was Lady Queen and they all lived happily together a good long time, Little Fawn being cared for and cosseted and allowed to leap around in the castle gardens. But as for the wicked stepmother, on whose account the children had first set off into the world, she reckoned that Little Sister had been torn to pieces by the wild animals of the forest, and Little Brother shot dead, as a fawn, by the king's huntsmen—so when she heard that they were now all so happy, and that everything had turned out so well for them, hatred and envy swelled in her heart, leaving her no peace, and she could think of nothing but how she might still bring down misfortune on the pair of them.

Now the woman's own true daughter was a girl as ugly as night, and with only one eye, and she reproached her mother, saying, "Ah, yes! being a queen—that's the sort of happiness I deserve."

"Bide you still," said the old woman, and calmed her down, saying, "When the time comes, I shall be there."

Now it so came about that eventually the queen brought a fine young boy into the world. The king was off hunting again, so the old witch took on the shape of a lady of the bedchamber, walked into the room where the sick queen was lying and said, "Come, madam, your bath is ready; it will do you good, help you recover your strength. Come along quickly, before it gets cold."

Her daughter was on hand as well and they carried the frail queen into the bathroom and laid her in the bath, then they shut the door and ran away. But they had so arranged it that the water in the bathroom was being heated hot as the fires of hell so that before long the beautiful young queen was suffocated.

When that was done the old woman got hold of her daughter, stuck a night-cap on her head, and put her in bed in place of the queen. She also gave her the form and figure of the queen, only she could do nothing to get her back her missing eye. (To make sure the king wouldn't notice this she had to lie down with that side of her head in the pillow.)

When the king got back in the evening and heard that he had a little son his heart filled with joy and he sought to go to his dear wife's bedside to see how she fared. The old woman, though, called out quickly, "Body and bones—don't touch the curtains. The queen can't have light just yet; she must be allowed to rest." So the king went away, not knowing it was a false queen lying in the bed.

When midnight came, however, and everything slept, the nurse who sat in the child's room, beside the cradle, and was the only one still awake, saw the door open and the real queen come in. She took her child from the cradle, laid him in her arms and fed him from her breast. Then she smoothed his little pillow, put him back in the cradle and covered him with his quilt. Nor did she forget the little fawn. She went to the corner where he was lying and stroked his back. Then, in absolute silence, she went back out through the door, and when, in the morning, the nurse asked the guards if anyone had been walking through the castle during the night they answered, "No; we haven't seen a soul." Thus it was that the queen came many nights, never speaking a word; and the nurse saw her every time, but did not trust herself to tell anyone about it.

Now after a good time had passed, a night came when the queen began to speak:

"How fares my child? How fares my fawn?
Two times I'll come and then nevermore."

The nurse said nothing to this, but when the queen had vanished, she went to the king and told him everything. And the king said, "God! God! what can be the meaning of this? Tonight I too shall watch beside the child." And in the evening he went into the child's room and around midnight the queen appeared again saying:

"How fares my child? How fares my fawn?
Once again I'll come and then nevermore."

53

And she tended the child as she always did and then she disappeared. The king did not trust himself to speak to her, but the next night he kept watch again, and once more she said:

"How fares my child? How fares my fawn?
This time I come and then nevermore."

And at this the king could not contain himself. He ran to her and said, "You cannot be anyone but my dearest wife," and she answered, "Yes, I am your dearest wife," and in that moment, by the grace of God, she came back to life, fresh-cheeked and bonny.

Then she told the king of the wickedness that the evil witch and her daughter had done to her. The king had both of them brought to judgement and their sentence was pronounced: the daughter was taken into the forest, where the wild beasts tore her to pieces; the witch was put in the fire and suffered a miserable death by burning. And when she was consumed to ashes the little fawn was transformed and once again took on his human shape. So Little Sister and Little Brother lived happily together to the end of their days.

The Frog King

or, Iron Henry

In the old days, when making wishes was still some use, there lived a king; and this king had three daughters. They were all of them beautiful, but the youngest was so beautiful that the sun in the sky (for all that he'd seen so much) marvelled every time he shone on her face.

Not far from the king's palace there stood a huge, dark forest, and in this forest, under an old linden tree, there was a well. Whenever the day was hot the king's youngest daughter would go out into the forest and sit herself down at the edge of the cool well; and if ever she got bored then she'd take out a golden ball, throw it up in the air and catch it again— and that was the toy she liked best of all.

Now once it so happened that the princess's golden ball didn't drop back into her little hands, held out there for it, but bounced away on the ground and straightway rolled into the water. The princess watched where it went, but the ball disappeared and the well was too deep, far too deep, for anyone to see right down to the bottom. So the princess began to cry, and she cried louder and louder and wasn't to be stilled.

And as she was weeping and wailing there, somebody called out to her, "What's to do with you, princess? You're crying fit to break a heart of stone."

She looked around to see where the voice was coming from and there she saw a frog, sticking his broad ugly head out of the water. "So it's you, is it, old Mr Paddlepat?" she said. "Well, if you must know, I'm crying for my golden ball that's fallen in the water."

"Then quiet yourself down and stop crying," answered the frog. "I'm well able to do something for you—but what'll you give me if I fish up your plaything again?"

"Oh you dear, kind frog," said the princess, "you can have whatever you like—my dresses, my pearls, my jewels, even the gold crown I'm wearing."

And the frog answered, "Dresses? Pearls? Jewels? Golden crowns? They're not things for me. But if you will love me, and if I were to be your friend and playfellow—sitting beside you at the table, eating out of your little golden plate, drinking out of your little mug, sleeping in your little bed—if you were to promise me all that, then I'd go down there at once and fetch up your golden ball for you."

"Yes, yes," said the princess, "yes; I promise everything you want if only you'll bring me back my ball." (But she thought to herself, "How that daft frog gabbles on, who can't do anything but sit in the water with the other frogs, croaking. No chance of him being anyone's friend.")

As soon as he'd got her promise, the frog ducked his head under the water, sank down, and then, after a while, came paddling up again. He had the ball in his mouth, and he threw it into the grass. The princess was overjoyed when she saw her beautiful plaything again. She picked it up and ran off with it. "Hey, wait!" called the frog, "take me with you! I can't run like that." But much good it did him, however loud he went with his "quark, quark-ing". She didn't listen to him, but hurried back home, and she soon forgot all about the poor old frog, who had no choice but to climb back into his well.

The next day, when, along with the king and all his court, the princess sat down at the table and was eating from her little golden plate, there came a "plitsch, platsch, plitsch, platsch" as something crept up the

The Frog King at the princess' bedside

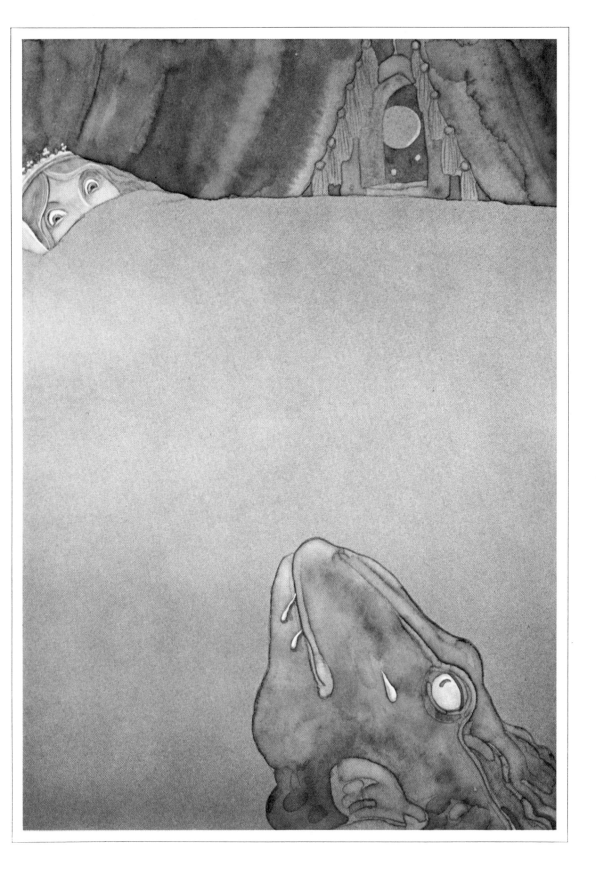

marble staircase, and when it got to the top it knocked at the door and called out, "Little youngest princess, let me in." She ran down the room, wanting to see who was outside, but when she opened the door, there was the frog sitting there. So she slammed the door shut and sat down again at the table, frightened out of her wits.

The king saw well enough how her heart was banging away, so he said, "Child, child, what are you frightened of? Did you see an ogre at the door, come to carry you off?"

"Oh no," she answered, "'twasn't an ogre but a beastly frog."

"And what did the frog want with you?"

"Oh papa, dear papa, when I was sitting by the well yesterday, playing, my golden ball fell into the water, and because I cried so much the frog fetched it out again for me, and because he made such a fuss about it I promised he should be my friend, but I never thought he'd be able to get out of his pond. Now he's out there and wants to come in to me." And while she spoke there was a second lot of knocking and a voice calling:

> "Little youngest princess
> Let me in.
> Have you forgotten what you did say
> Down by the well's edge yesterday?
> Little youngest princess
> Let me in."

Then the king said, "What you have promised you must keep. Go and let him in."

So she went and opened the door and the frog hopped along at her feet back to her chair. There he sat down and called out, "Lift me up to you," but she hesitated until the king ordered it. But once the frog was on the chair he wanted to be on the table, and when he got there he said, "Now push your little golden plate a bit nearer, so that we can both eat out of it together." And she did so—although you could see that she didn't like doing it.

The frog made a good meal, but the princess's every mouthful stuck in her throat. Eventually, though, the frog said, "I've had enough and I'm tired; now carry me up to your little room, turn down your silken bed, and we'll go to sleep together."

Then the princess began to cry again, frightened of the clammy frog that she didn't trust herself to touch and that was now to sleep in her beautiful clean little bed. But the king was angry, and said, "Those who help you in trouble are not to be scorned later."

So she picked him up between her finger and thumb, carried him up and put him down in a corner. But when she'd got into bed he came creeping up and said, "I'm tired. I'll sleep as well as you do. Pick me up or I'll tell your father." Then she turned bitterly angry, picked him up and hurled him against the wall as hard as she could. "Now you can go to sleep, you beastly little frog!"

But as he fell to the ground he was a frog no more, but a prince with kindly, beautiful eyes—and he was, as her father desired, her dear friend and husband. Then he told her how he had been enchanted by a wicked witch and how no one but she alone could free him from the well; and tomorrow they should go together to his kingdom.

Then they went back to sleep, and the next morning, when the sun had woken them, a coach came up, drawn by eight white horses, with white plumes and golden traces, and behind stood the young king's servant who was known as Faithful Henry. (Faithful Henry had been so overcome with grief when his master was changed into a frog that he had caused three iron bands to be fastened round his heart so that it shouldn't burst from sorrow and despair.) Now, though, the coach was to take the young king to his kingdom. Faithful Henry handed in both king and bride, and climbed up behind once more, full of joy at his master's release. And after they'd driven on for a way the prince heard a cracking, splintering noise behind them, as though something had broken. So he turned round and cried out:

"Henry the coach is shaking to pieces!"

"Not the coach, Lord, breaking to pieces—
  'Tis but a band round my heart,
  Fastened when we had to part—
  The blackest days that time can tell
  When you were Frog inside the well."

59

Once more, and yet once more the splitting noises came as they travelled along, and the prince thought each time it was the carriage breaking—but it was only the iron bands round Faithful Henry's heart bursting asunder because his master was free again and happy.

Little Snow-White

Once, long ago, deep in winter, when the snow-flakes fell from heaven like feathers, a queen sat beside a window that was framed in black ebony; and the queen was sewing. And as she sewed there, looking out across the snow, she pricked her finger with the needle and three drops of blood fell down into the snow. And because the red looked so beautiful in the white snow she thought to herself, "What if I were to have a child as white as snow, as red as blood, and as black as the wood of this window-frame." And soon afterwards she gave birth to a little daughter, who was as white as snow, as red as blood, and whose hair was as black as ebony—and because of this she was called Little Snow-White. And as the child was born, the queen died.

A year or so later the king took another wife for himself. She was a beautiful woman, but she was proud and arrogant, and she could not bear to be outdone by anyone for beauty. She had a marvellous mirror and when she stepped in front of it, looked at herself and said:

"Mirror, mirror on the wall,
  Who is the fairest one of all?"

then the mirror replied:

"Lady Queen, you are the fairest one of all."

So she was content, for she knew that the mirror told the truth.

Little Snow-White, however, was growing up and every day growing more beautiful, and when she was seven years old she was as beautiful as the light of day and more beautiful than the queen herself. So, when the queen next asked the mirror:

"Mirror, mirror on the wall,
   Who is the fairest one of all?"

the mirror answered:

"Lady Queen you are the fairest here,
   But Snow-White is a thousand times more fair."

Then the queen was horrified and turned yellow and green from spite. And from that moment on, whenever she saw Little Snow-White her heart would turn over in her body so great was her hatred for the girl. And Pride and Envy grew like weeds inside her, bigger and bigger, so that she could not rest by day or by night.

So one day she called a huntsman to her and said, "Take the child out there to the forest, I never want to have sight of her again. Kill her, and bring me her lungs and her liver as proof that you have done it."

The huntsman obeyed and took Little Snow-White off—but when he had drawn his hunting-knife and made to drive it into her innocent heart she began to weep and said, "Ah, huntsman, dear huntsman, let me live. I will run away into the wild forest and never come home again."

And because she was so beautiful, the huntsman had pity and said, "Run away then, you poor little thing." He thought to himself, "The wild creatures of the forest will eat you up soon enough." Yet, even so, it was as if a stone had fallen from his heart, because he did not have to kill her. And since a young wild boar came trotting along just at that moment, he stabbed him, cut out his lungs and his liver and brought them back to the queen for his proof. Then the palace cook was made to stew them up with plenty of salt and the evil queen ate them and believed that she had eaten Little Snow-White's lungs and liver.

As for the poor child, she was now alone and deserted in the great forest and was so frightened that she looked round at all the leaves on the trees and did not know what to do to save herself. So she began to run, and she ran and ran, over sharp stones and through thorns, and the wild creatures sprang past her but didn't hurt her. She ran for as long as her feet would carry her, until, towards evening, she saw a tiny little house and went inside to rest. Everything in the little house was tiny, but more neat and clean than words can tell. A little table laid with a white cloth was standing there, set out with seven little plates, and beside each plate there was a little spoon, and there were also seven little knives, seven little forks and seven little mugs. Along the wall there were seven little beds, one by one in a row, each one covered with a snow-white sheet.

Because she was so hungry and thirsty, Little Snow-White ate some of the bread and salad from each of the little plates, and drank a drop of wine from each of the little mugs—for she did not want to take everything from one place only. Then, because she was so tired, she lay down in one of the little beds—but the little beds did not suit her. One was too long, another too short, until eventually the seventh one was just right, and there she stayed lying, said her prayers, and fell asleep.

When it was quite dark, the lords and masters of this little mansion returned home: seven dwarfs who spent their days digging and burrowing after metal inside the mountains. They lit their seven little lamps and since it was now light in the little house they saw that someone had been there for things were not as neat and tidy as when they'd left them.

The first dwarf said, "Who's been sitting in my little chair?"; the second, "Who's been eating from my little plate?"; the third, "Who's been nibbling my bit of bread?"; the fourth, "Who's been eating my little salad?"; the fifth, "Who's been poking with my little fork?"; the sixth, "Who's been cutting with my little knife?"; the seventh, "Who's been drinking from my little mug?"

Then the first dwarf looked about him and saw that there was a little hollow in his bed, and he said, "Who's been getting on my little bed?"

and the others came running and cried out, "Yes, someone's been lying in my bed too!" But when the seventh looked at his bed he saw Little Snow-White, lying there and sleeping. He called to the others and they came running up and cried out with amazement. They fetched their seven little lamps and let the light fall on Little Snow-White.

"By the good Lord! By the good Lord!" they cried. "What a beautiful child!" and they were so overjoyed that they did not wake her but let her go on sleeping in the little bed. (The seventh dwarf had to sleep with the others—one hour with each of them—then the night was over.)

When it was morning Little Snow-White woke up, and when she saw the seven dwarfs she was terrified. But the dwarfs were kindly and asked her, "What's your name?"

"My name's Little Snow-White," she answered.

"How did you get to this house of ours?" they went on—and she told them that her stepmother had wanted to kill her, but that the huntsman had spared her life and that she had run the whole day long until at last she had come upon their little house.

Then the dwarfs said, "If you will look after the house for us—cook and make the beds and do the washing and sewing and knitting, and if you will keep everything neat and clean, then you can stay with us and you shall want for nothing."

"Yes," said Little Snow-White, "with all my heart," and she stayed there with them. She kept the house in order for them, and every morning they would go off to the mountains, looking for iron and gold, and every evening they would return, and then their suppers had to be ready for them. But since the girl was on her own all through the day the kindly dwarfs warned her, "Look out for your stepmother. She'll know soon enough that you're here. Don't let anyone in."

Now—as for this queen—once she'd eaten what she took to be Little Snow-White's lungs and liver she thought of nothing more than that she was once again the most beautiful person in the world. She stepped in front of her mirror and said:

> "Mirror, mirror on the wall,
>   Who is the fairest one of all?"

The dwarfs find Snow-White

and the mirror answered:

> "Lady Queen, you are the fairest here;
>   But over the hills, in the house of the dwarfs
>   Snow-White is a thousand times more fair."

Then she was horrified, for she knew that the mirror could not tell a lie, and she realised that the huntsman had deceived her and that Little Snow-White was still alive.

So she thought and thought of ways to kill Snow-White, for her envy would give her no rest as long as she knew that she was not the most beautiful woman in the whole country. And when at last she was done with thinking she stained her face and dressed herself as an old pedlar-woman so that no one could tell who she was. In this disguise she walked over the seven hills to the house of the seven dwarfs, knocked at the door and cried out, "Good things for sale! Fine things for sale!"

And Little Snow-White peeped out of the window and called, "Good morning, old lady, what are you selling?"

"Good things, fine things," she answered. "Ribbons and laces every colour you can think of," and she brought out a lace that was woven of many-coloured silk.

"Well," thought Little Snow-White, "I can let in an honest-looking old woman like that," and she unbolted the door and bought the pretty lace for herself.

"My dear child," said the old woman, "what a sight you are! Come along, let me lace you properly."

Little Snow-White was a picture of modesty. She stood in front of the old woman and let her lace her bodice with the new ribbon—but the old woman laced quick and she laced tight so that Little Snow-White lost her breath and fell down as if dead.

"There," said the old woman, "you *were* the fairest in the land," and she hurried out.

Not long afterwards, at evening, the seven dwarfs came home; but how terrified they were when they saw their beloved Little Snow-White lying on the ground, neither stirring nor moving, just as though she were dead! They raised her up, and since they saw that she was too tightly laced up they cut the ribbons in two. So it was that she began to breathe and gradually came back to life again.

When the dwarfs heard what had happened, they said, "Depend upon it, the old pedlar was nobody but that devilish queen. Look out and don't let anyone in at all when we're not at home with you."

As for the evil woman though, when she got home she stood before her mirror and asked:

"Mirror, mirror on the wall,
Who is the fairest one of all?"

and the mirror answered as before:

"Lady Queen, you are the fairest here;
But over the hills, in the house of the dwarfs
Snow-White is a thousand times more fair."

When she heard that she was so horrified that all the blood fled from her heart, for she saw well enough that Little Snow-White had come back to life again. "Very well," she said, "I will devise something that will destroy you utterly," and with powers of witchcraft that she possessed she made a poisonous comb. Then she disguised herself, taking the form of yet another old woman, and so she travelled, over the seven hills to the house of the seven dwarfs, knocked at the door and cried, "Good things for sale! Fine things for sale!"

Little Snow-White looked out and said, "Go away, I'm not allowed to let anyone in."

"But nobody will mind you looking, will they?" said the old woman, she drew out the poisoned comb and held it up to be seen. The child was so taken with it that she let herself be deceived and opened the door.

When they had settled the bargain the old woman said, "Now I will comb your hair properly,"—and poor Little Snow-White thought nothing of it and let the old woman do so. But hardly had she stuck the comb in her hair than the poison began working and the girl fell down senseless. "You paragon of beauty," said the evil woman, "that should have done for you," and she went away.

Fortunately, though, it was almost evening-time, and when the seven dwarfs came back to their house, and saw Little Snow-White lying on the ground as though dead they suspected that her stepmother had come again. They hunted about and found the poisoned comb and scarcely had they pulled it out than Little Snow-White came to her senses and told them what had happened. Then they warned her once again to be on her guard and never to open the door to anyone.

When the queen returned home she stood before the mirror and said:

"Mirror, mirror on the wall,
    Who is the fairest one of all?"

and the mirror answered her as before:

"Lady Queen, you are the fairest here;
    But over the hills, in the house of the dwarfs
    Snow-White is a thousand times more fair."

When she heard the mirror say these words she trembled and shook with rage. "Little Snow-White shall die," she cried, "even if it costs me my own life too." Thereupon she went into a secret, lonely chamber, where no one ever came, and she made there a poisonous, poisonous apple. From the outside it looked beautiful—white-fleshed and red-cheeked—so that anyone who saw it would long for it, but whoever ate even a morsel of it was doomed to death.

When the apple was finished the queen stained her face and disguised herself as a peasant woman and walked over the seven hills to the house of the seven dwarfs. She knocked at the door and Little Snow-White leaned out of the window and said, "I am not to let anyone in; the seven dwarfs have forbidden it."

"Well, that's all the same to me," answered the peasant woman. "I'll soon be rid of these apples of mine. But look— I'll give you one."

"No," said Little Snow-White, "I'm not allowed to take anything at all."

"What!" said the old woman, "are you afraid of being poisoned? Look here. Let me cut this apple in two and you eat the red half while I eat the white." For the apple was so cunningly made that only the red cheek was poisoned.

Little Snow-White longed for the beautiful apple, and when she saw that the peasant woman was eating it she could not contain herself any more. She stretched out her hand and took the poisoned half. But scarcely had a single bite gone into her mouth than she fell down dead to the ground. Then the queen looked at her with a terrible countenance, burst into wild laughter and said, "White as snow, red as blood, black as ebony! This time the dwarfs will not wake you up again." And when she got home she asked her mirror:

"Mirror, mirror on the wall,
Who is the fairest one of all?"

and at last the mirror answered:

"Lady Queen, you are the fairest one of all,"

so that her envious heart was now at rest, at least so far as ever an envious heart can be at rest.

When the little dwarfs came back to their house that evening they found Little Snow-White lying on the ground, and not a breath left in her body. She was dead. They raised her up, looked to see if they could find anything poisonous, unlaced her, combed her hair, washed her with water and with wine, but it was all to no purpose. Dead the dear child was, and dead she stayed.

They laid her body on a bier and all seven sat round it and wept—and they wept for three long days. Then they looked to bury her, but she still seemed hale as a living person, still had her beautiful rosy cheeks. So they said to each other, "We cannot bury such a thing in the black earth," and they had made a transparent coffin of glass, so that she could be looked at from all sides, and they laid her in it and wrote her name upon it in golden letters, saying that she was the daughter of a king. Then they set down the coffin outside on the mountain with one of them always beside it to watch over it. And even the animals came and wept for Little Snow-White—first an owl, then a raven and last of all a little dove.

For a long, long time Little Snow-White lay in her coffin, unchanging, just as if she slept: as white as snow, as red as blood, and with hair as black as ebony. But it so happened that a young prince found his way into the forest and sought to spend the night at the house of the seven dwarfs. He saw the coffin on the mountain, with beautiful Snow-White inside it, and he read what was written on it in letters of gold. Then he said to the dwarfs, "Let me have this coffin—I will give you whatever you want for it."

But the dwarfs answered, "We would not part with it for all the gold in the world."

Then the prince said, "Well, give it to me for I cannot live without being able to see Snow-White. I will honour and serve her as if she were my dearest love."

When he said that the kindly dwarfs took pity on him and gave him the coffin, and the young prince had his servants set it on their shoulders to carry it away. It so happened, though, that they stumbled over a tussock and, because of the jolt, the poisonous bite of apple that Little Snow-White had taken jerked out of her throat. And it was only a moment before she opened her eyes, raised up the lid of the coffin, and sat up alive again.

"In Heaven's name, where am I?" she cried, and the young prince, overcome with joy, answered, "You are with me." And he told her everything that had happened, saying, "I love you more than everything in the world. Come home to my father's castle. You shall be my wife." And Little Snow-White looked at him kindly and went with him, and their wedding was celebrated with great magnificence and splendour.

Now Little Snow-White's devilish stepmother was among those who were invited to the feast. When she had dressed herself in her most beautiful robes she stepped before her mirror and said:

"Mirror, mirror on the wall,
    Who is the fairest one of all?"

and the mirror answered:

"Lady Queen, you are the fairest here,
    But the young queen is a thousand times more fair."

Then the wicked woman spat out a curse and became so frantic, so frantic, that she did not know what to do with herself. First she would not go to the wedding at all; but then she could not rest with thinking of it—she had to go—she had to see the new young queen. And when she entered the hall, she recognised Little Snow-White and she stood there and could not move for fear and horror. But iron slippers had already been set to heat over a charcoal fire and these were carried in with tongs and put in front of her. And she had to step into the red-hot shoes and dance and dance until she fell down dead to the ground.

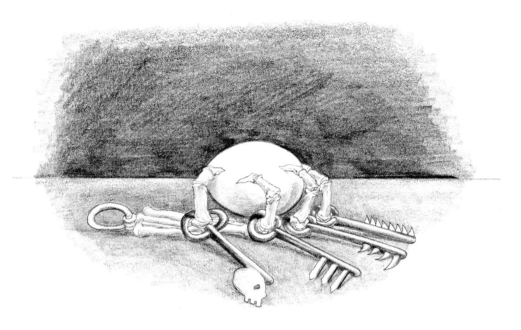

Fitcher's Bird

Once upon a time there was a wizard, who used to take on the looks of a poor man and go round the houses begging—and he used to catch pretty girls. Nobody found out where he took them off to, because none of them ever came home to tell the tale.

Now, one day he came past the door of a man who had three beautiful daughters. As usual he was looking like a poor, clapped-out beggarman and he carried a wallet at his back for collecting alms in. He asked for a bite to eat, and when the eldest daughter came out and tried to hand him a piece of bread he just touched her and she had to jump into the bag. Then he made off, with strides a good sight longer than a beggarman's, and carried her to his house which stood in the middle of a gloomy forest. Everything in the house was wonderful. He gave her whatever she wished for, and said, "Come, my treasure, you will be happy living here with me, you've got everything your heart desires."

Well, that went on for a few days, then he said, "Now I must go away on a journey and leave you alone for a little while. Here are the keys of the house—you can go all over it—look at anything you like—but not in

72

the one room that is opened with this little key. That I forbid you on pain of death." And he gave her an egg as well, saying, "Look after this egg carefully. Best of all, carry it round with you all the time, for if it were to get lost a terrible calamity would follow." So she took the keys and the egg and promised to manage everything properly.

Once he had left she went through the house from top to bottom and looked at everything. The rooms were all a-glitter with silver and gold and she reckoned never to have seen such magnificence before. Then, at last, she came to the forbidden door. She tried to force herself to go past it, but her curiosity gave her no peace. She looked at the key. It was just like any other key. She poked it into the lock and turned it—ever so little—and pam!—the door sprang open. But what did she see when she went in? There in the middle of the room stood a great, bloody basin and inside the basin were dead people, all chopped up. Beside it there was a block of wood with a glittering axe stuck in it. The girl was so terribly frightened that the egg, which she was holding in her hand, tumbled into the basin. She dragged it out again and wiped off the blood—but all in vain. The moment it was gone it appeared again. She wiped it and rubbed it but she couldn't do away with it.

Soon after this the man returned from his journey, and the first thing he asked for was the key and the egg. She handed them over to him—trembling all the while—and he saw at once from the red stains that she had been in the Room of Blood.

"Since you have gone into the chamber against my will," he said, "you must now go into it against your own. Your life is finished," and he threw her down, dragged her into the room by her hair, struck off her head on the block and chopped her in pieces so that her blood streamed all over the floor. Then he threw her into the basin with the others.

"Now I'll fetch the second one," said the wizard, and once more he took on the looks of a poor man and went past the house begging. Then the second daughter brought him a piece of bread and he caught her like the first, just by touching her, and he carried her off. Well, it went no better for her than for her sister. She let herself be overcome by curiosity, opened the Room of Blood, looked inside, and paid for it with her life when the man returned.

73

So now he went for the third daughter—but she was a tricky, crafty one. When he'd given her the key and the egg and gone off on his journey she first of all set the egg by carefully in a safe place and then went round looking at the house. Finally she came to the forbidden chamber and—oh! oh! oh! oh!—what did she see? There were her two darling sisters, lying in the basin, woefully slaughtered and chopped in pieces. But she set about things and assembled together all the bits of their corpses and laid them out properly—head, body, arms and legs. And when nothing else was missing the limbs began to move and joined themselves up, each to each, and the two girls opened their eyes and came alive again. And how they rejoiced—hugging and kissing each other no end!

When he returned, the man demanded the key and the egg as usual, and since he couldn't find any trace of blood there he said, "You have proved yourself. You shall be my bride," and that meant that he now had no more power over her and must do what she wanted.

"Very well," said she, "before you do anything else you must take a basket of gold to my mother and father and, what's more, carry it on your own back. Meantime I'll arrange the wedding."

Then she ran to her two sisters, whom she'd hidden in a little side-room, and she said, "Now's the time when I can rescue you. This monster's going to carry you home himself, but once you get there send help for me." And she put the two of them in a basket and covered them up with the gold so that you couldn't see anything of them at all. Then she called in the wizard and said, "Now, off you go with this basket. But just to make sure you don't hang around on the way, sitting down to rest, I'll be standing at my little window, keeping an eye on you."

The wizard heaved the basket on to his back and set off. But it weighed him down so heavily that the sweat began to pour down his face. So he sat himself down to rest for a bit, but straight away one of the girls in the basket called out, "I'm watching you through my little window! I can see you sitting there. Get on with you!" And he reckoned it was his bride calling out like that, so he got up again. After a bit though he needed another rest, but the voice came: "I'm watching you through my little window! I can see you sitting there. Get on with you!" And every time he stood still the voice called, and he had to go on, till at last,

breathless and groaning, he brought the basket with the gold and the two girls to their parents' home.

Back at his own house though, the bride was arranging the wedding celebrations, and she had all the wizard's friends invited. Then she took a skull, with great grinning teeth, set it about with finery and a garland of flowers, carried it up to the attic window and had it look forth. Then, when everything was ready, she jumped into a tub of honey, cut up her eiderdown and rolled in the feathers so that she came to look like a weird bird and no one could recognise her. Then she left the house, and, on her way down the road she met a party of wedding-guests who asked:

"You, Fitcher's Bird, how came you here?"
"From Fitze Fitcher's house I have come here."
"What did you see the young bride doing there?"
"She's turned the whole place upside down
    And now from the attic window she looks down."

At last she met the bridegroom, wandering slowly back. Like the others, he asked:

"You, Fitcher's Bird, how came you here?"
"From Fitze Fitcher's house I have come here."
"What did you see my young bride doing there?"
"She's turned the whole place upside down
    And now from the attic window she looks down."

The bridegroom looked up and saw the fancy skull and reckoned it was his bride and nodded to her and waved her a friendly greeting. But when he'd gone into the house, along with his guests, the brothers and all the relations of the bride arrived, sent to rescue her. They shut all the doors of the house so that no one could escape and set fire to it so that the wizard and all his crew were burnt.

The Merry Tale of
the Clever Little Tailor

Once upon a time there was a princess, and a mighty proud one at that. If anyone came to court her then she'd give him a riddle to guess and if he couldn't guess it she'd make fun of him and send him packing. What's more she gave out that whoever did guess her riddle then he was the one she'd marry, and anyone could try that wanted to.

Well one day, three tailors met up with each other and the two older ones reckoned that they'd strung together so many stitches in their time, and done so well by it, that they couldn't help do well here too—while as for the youngest, well, he was nobbut a little, good-for-nothing fancy-man, who hadn't got the first idea how to do his job, but he reckoned he was bound to have good luck, because if he didn't get good luck here he wouldn't get it anywhere else.

At the start the two others said to him, "Why don't you just stay at home? You won't get on much with your bit of a brain." But the little tailor wouldn't let himself be put off and said that since he'd set his mind to the matter he'd shift for himself. And off he went with them as if he owned the whole world.

So all three called on the princess and said she should ask them her riddle, "For," said they, "the right folk have turned up now, with wits so fine you could almost thread a needle with them."

Then the princess said, "I've got two kinds of hair on my head; what colour are they?"

"If that's all you want to know," said the first tailor, "that's easy. They're black and white, like the cloth we call pepper and salt."

"Wrong," said the princess, "now let's hear from number two."

Then the second tailor said, "No, they're not black and white, they're brown and red like my old father's Sunday weskit."

"Wrong again," said the princess, "now let's hear from number three, he looks as though he knows what he's about."

Then the little tailor stepped up smartly and said, "The princess has got gold and silver hair on her head—those are the two colours." And when the princess heard that she turned white as a sheet and almost tumbled over with fright, for the little tailor had hit the mark, while she'd been thinking that no one in the whole wide world would be able to do so.

But once she'd got her courage back, she said, "That's all very well, but don't think you've won me just yet—there's still one thing you've got to do. Down below in the stables there's a bear, and you're to spend the night with him. If you're still alive when I get up in the morning then we shall be wed." (For she thought by this to be well rid of the tailor, since the bear had never let anyone off alive once he'd got him in his clutches. But the little tailor didn't take fright at that and said comfortably enough: "Courage up is half the battle.")

Now when evening had come they brought the little tailor down to the bear and this bear was all ready to be up to give the fellow a warm welcome with his claws. "Steady, steady," said the little tailor to himself, "I'll deal with you soon enough," and very calmly, as if he hadn't a care in the world, he pulled a handful of walnuts out of his pocket, cracked the shells with his teeth and ate the nuts.

When the bear saw this he decided that he'd like some nuts as well.

Dancing lessons from a clever tailor

So the little tailor reached into his pocket and brought out another handful—only this time they weren't nuts but pebbles. The bear stuffed them in his mouth, but try as he would he couldn't crack them. "Ay, ay," he thought, "what sort of a cloth-head are you? Why can't you get your teeth into these nuts?" and he said to the little tailor: "Now then, can you crack me these nuts?"

"There," said the little tailor, "that shows what kind of a chap you are—great big mouth like yours and you can't crack a few little nuts," and he took the stones, did a quick switch and popped a nut in his mouth. Crack! It was in half.

"I must try this again," said the bear, "it looks easy enough to me." So the little tailor gives him some more pebbles and the bear works away at them, biting with all his strength. But you know as well as I do that he had no luck.

When this game was over the little tailor brought out a fiddle from under his coat and played over a couple of pieces. When the bear heard the music he couldn't keep still but got up and started to dance; and after he'd danced for a bit he found the whole thing so pleasing that he said to the little tailor: "Hey! how easy is it then to play the fiddle?"

"Child's play," said the little tailor. "Look I put my fingers on the strings like this, and I take the bow like this and away we go—hopla, hopla—over the hills and far away."

"So," said the bear, "fiddling; that's something I'd like to do so that I could dance whenever I wanted. What do you reckon? Will you give me a lesson?"

"With all my heart," said the little tailor, "so long as you're apt. But let's have a look at those claws; they're a sight too long; I'll have to cut your nails for you." So he brought along a vice and the bear put his paws inside; then the little tailor screwed them in tight and said, "Now wait till I get the scissors," and he left the bear to growl as much as it wanted, settled down on a bundle of straw in the corner and went to sleep.

That night, when the princess heard the bear growling and making such a fuss, she couldn't think but what he was growling for joy because he'd given the little tailor his comeuppance. Next morning, then, she got up without a care in the world, but when she takes a look in the stable what does she see but the little old tailor standing there as bonny as a fish in a brook. Well, since everybody knew about her having promised to marry him there was nothing left for her to say against it and the king had a carriage brought round to take the two of them to church. Once they'd climbed aboard the two other tailors (who were false-hearted fellows and had no great love for their comrade) went along to the stable and unloosed the bear. The bear who, by this time, was pretty cross ran after the carriage.

The princess heard him snuffing and growling, which properly frightened her, and she cried out, "Ow! the bear's behind us and he's coming after you!" But the little tailor was a sharp one; he stood on his head, stuck his legs out of the window and shouted, "Watch out for the vice! If you don't clear off you'll be inside again." And when the bear saw that, he turned and ran off.

So the little old tailor drove on quietly to the church and the princess was wed with him and they lived together happy as a pair of larks. And if you don't believe that, it'll cost you a shilling.

The Sad Tale of Clever Elsie

There was a man had a daughter they all called Clever Elsie. When she was of age her Dad said, "She must be wed," and her Ma said, "Ay, if anyone comes as 'll have her."

Well, before long, a feller comes from a good way off, Jack b'name, and asks for her—but they had to satisfy him Clever Elsie was a real sharp 'un.

"Oh, ay," said her Dad, "she's got brains in her head right enough," and her Ma said, "That's it. She can see the wind blowing down the snicket and hear the flies coughing."

"Well that's good," said Jack, "because if she's not real sharp, I'm not having her."

Now while they were sitting at table after supper her Ma said, "Elsie, run down the cellar and fetch some beer." So Clever Elsie took the jug off the wall and went down to the cellar, joggling the stopper, clacketty clack, as she went, to pass the time. When she got below she fetched a chair along and set it in front of the barrel so that she didn't need to bend down, which might do something nasty to her back and bring about

who knows what damage. Then she put the jug down in front of her and turned on the spigot. But while the beer was running into the jug she wouldn't let her eyes be still, gazed up at the wall, and, after a lot of peering backwards and forwards she spotted a pick-axe right above her head, stuck there by the masons and forgotten.

Then Clever Elsie began to cry, and said, "If I get that Jack and we have a child and he grows up and we send him down the cellar to draw some beer then that chopper'll fall on his head and do for him." And she sat there weeping and wailing fit to bust over this forthcoming disaster.

The folks upstairs stayed waiting for their beer, but Clever Elsie never came back. So her Ma said to the kitchen-maid, "Now you go down to the cellar and see what's keeping Elsie." So the maid went and found Elsie sitting by the barrel wailing.

"Elsie, what are you crying for?" asked the maid.

"Aaoow!" answered Elsie, "who wouldn't cry? If I get that Jack and we have a child and he grows up and we send him down the cellar to draw some beer then that chopper'll fall on his head and do for him."

Then the kitchen-maid said, "My, there's a clever Elsie!" and she sat down beside her and began to cry over the calamity too.

After a while, what with the kitchen-maid not coming back and everyone upstairs panting for their beer, the man said to the serving-boy, "Now you go down to the cellar and see what's keeping Elsie and the maid." So the lad went down and there were Clever Elsie and the maid sitting weeping side by side. So he asked, "What are you crying for?"

"Aaoow!" answered Elsie, "who wouldn't cry? If I get that Jack and we have a child and he grows up and we send him down the cellar to draw some beer then that chopper'll fall on his head and do for him."

Then the boy said, "My, there's a clever Elsie," and he sat down beside her and began yelling like mad.

Upstairs they waited for the serving-boy, but when he never came back the man said to his wife, "Now you go down the cellar and see what's keeping Elsie." So Ma went down and found all three of them wailing for grief, and when she asked why, Clever Elsie told her all about the child who might well be done for by the chopper when he'd grown up enough to draw the beer and had the chopper fall on his head.

So Ma likewise says, "My, there's a clever Elsie," and she sat down and cried along with the rest of them.

Upstairs the man waited a little while yet, but when his wife never came back and his thirst got real terrible he said, "Well, I'd best go down the cellar myself and see what's keeping Elsie." But when he got down the cellar with all of them sitting alongside each other weeping, and when he heard the reason: about what was coming to this child of Elsie's, that she might bring into the world at some stage, and that might be killed stone dead by the chopper, if, at the time when it fell down, he happened to be sitting underneath it drawing beer, then he shouted, "My, what a clever Elsie!" and he sat down and cried along with the rest of them.

The young feller who'd come courting stayed on alone upstairs for a good long time, but since nobody seemed to want to come back he said to himself, "They're all waiting for you down there. You'd better go down and see what they're up to." And when he got down there, there were the five of them wailing and taking on, each one louder than the next, enough to break your heart. "What sort of calamity's happened here then?" he asked.

"Aah! Jack my love," said Elsie, "When we get wed and have a child, and he grows up, and mebbe we send him down here to draw something to drink, then that chopper up there could bash his head in if it fell down. Who wouldn't cry about that?"

"Well, now," said Jack, "nobody in my house needs more brains than that—since you're such a clever Elsie you're just the one for me," and he grabbed her by the hand and took her back upstairs and married her.

After they'd been together a while, Jack said, "Woman, I'm going off to do some work and earn a bit of money. You go into the field and cut the corn so we can have some bread."

"All right, Jack love, I'll do it." So after he'd gone she boiled up some meal and took it with her into the field. When she got to the corn she said to herself, "What'll I do? Cut first or eat first? Eeh—I'll eat first." So she ate up the meal, and since she was now full to busting, she said to herself again, "What'll I do? Cut first or sleep first? Eeh—I'll sleep first," and she lay down in the corn and slept.

Jack got back and was home a good long time, but no sign of Elsie. So he said, "My, there's a Clever Elsie—she's so busy she won't come home to eat." By the time evening had come though, and she still wasn't back, Jack went out to see how much she'd cut—but, of course, nothing was cut and there was Elsie lying in the corn sleeping. So Jack hurried home quick and fetched a bird-net, all hung about with little bells, and he draped it round her, and she went on sleeping. Then he ran back, shut the front-door and sat down in his chair and got on with his work.

Eventually, when it was all dark, Clever Elsie woke up, and when she got to her feet there was a great rattling, and at every step she took a tinkling of bells. That gave her a bit of a fright and she got all confused over whether she really was Clever Elsie and she said, "Am I? or aren't I?"—but she couldn't decide what the answer was and she stood for a while not knowing what to do. At last she thought, "I'll go up the house and ask if it's me or if it isn't me—they're sure to know." So she ran to the front-door, but it was shut. So she banged at the window and called out "Hey Jack! is Elsie there?"

"Yes," said Jack, "she's here."

Then she got really frightened and said, "Lordy, Lordy—then I'm not me," and she went to another door, but when folk heard the little bells ringing they wouldn't open up and she couldn't come by any sort of lodging. So she ran off out of the village and she's not been seen since.

Lazy 'Arry; Sunny Jim; and Skinny Lizzie:
Three Stories

'Arry was lazy—and for all 'e'd got nothing to do but lug 'is goat orf to the field every day 'e moaned on when 'e came 'ome in the evenings after work. "Strewth," 'e used to say, "it's an 'ard job, a perishin' weary business, lugging a goat like this orf to the fields every year, from one Michaelmas round to the next. It's not as if you could lie down an' 'ave a bit of a kip neither—oh, no!—you've got to keep your eyes open to see she don't spoil the new trees, or get through an 'edge into someone's garden, or just simply run orf. 'Ow can you get any peace with all that going on? Where's the fun in all that?" An' 'e sat 'imself down, got 'is wits together, and considered 'ow 'e could be rid of 'is load.

For a long time all 'is brooding went for nothing, until suddenly it came to 'im like a flash of greased lightning. "I know what I'll do," 'e shouted. "I'll get fixed up with Fat Trina—she's got a goat as well an' she can cart mine orf along with 'ers, then I won't 'ave anything else to worry about."

So 'Arry 'eaves 'imself up, sets 'is weary bones a-going, and walks acrorst the street ('e didn't 'ave to go any further, because that's where Fat Trina's parents lived), and 'e straightway asks for the 'and of their 'ighly esteemed and 'ardworking daughter. Well, 'er mum and dad didn't stop long to think about *that*. "Like for like" was their opinion and they agreed straight away. And so Fat Trina got 'erself joined in 'oly wedlock to 'Arry and 'ad to take out both the goats, while 'Arry put 'is feet up at 'ome, where the only work 'e 'ad to recover from was the work of being so lazy. Now and then, though, 'e'd go out with Trina as well, saying, "I'm only doing all this work because it's nice when you leave orf; otherwise you lose your taste for a bit of kip."

I'm sorry to say though, that Fat Trina was just as lazy as 'e was. "'Arry, my love," she said one day, "what's the good of us drudging away like this, when there's no need—wasting the best years of our lives? Wouldn't it be better if we gave those two goats to the bloke next door—after all they keep on waking us up in the morning just when we're warm and comfy—and 'e can swap us a bee'ive for 'em? We could put a bee'ive in that sunny patch be'ind the 'ouse and then we needn't worry about it any more. Bees don't want watching. You don't have to lug them orf to the fields—they all go flying about the place, find their own way back 'ome and collect all that lovely 'oney without us 'aving to do anything about it at all."

"That's what I call the word of a sensible woman," answered 'Arry. "It's an idea we'll get to work on straight away—and, what's more, the 'oney'll taste better than goat's milk, it'll do us more good than goat's milk, and it won't go orf so quick as goat's milk."

The bloke next door was glad to swap the two goats for a bee'ive. And as for the bees, they flew busily backwards and forwards from first thing in the morning to last thing in the evening, filling the 'ive with the most beautiful 'oney, so that—come the autumn—'Arry was able to take out a whole great jar of the stuff.

They put this jar on a shelf that was fixed up on one of the walls of their bedroom and since they were scared it might be stolen or the mice might get at it Trina laid in a good stout 'azel stick and put it down by the bed so they could catch 'old of it without 'aving to trouble 'emselves to get up. Then they could drive orf the unwanted company while they were still in bed.

Lazy 'Arry didn't like 'aving to get up before mid-day. "People who get up early," 'e said, "use up all their vital juices." Then one morning, while 'e lay under the eiderdown in broad daylight, recovering from 'is long sleep, 'e said to 'is missus, "You women are all too fond of a bit of something sweet, and I can see that you've been at the 'oney. Well, before the 'ole lot's been eaten up by you on the sly it'd be better to trade it for a goose with a little gosling."

"But we can't do that," said Trina, "till we've got a boy to look after it. Do you expect me to fuss around with a lot of little geese, wasting all me 'ealth and strength when there's no need?"

"Do you really think," said 'Arry, "that kids'll look after geese? Kids these days don't do as they're told any more. They go orf and do as they like, because they think they're cleverer than what their parents are—just like that young feller with the cow and the blackbirds." (You'll 'ear about him in a moment.)

"Gar," said Trina, "'e'll catch it if 'e doesn't do what I tell 'im. I'll take a stick to 'im and tan 'is 'ide like fury. Just you see 'Arry," she shouted—all worked up and grabbing the stick that they used for chasing the mice, "just you see, I'll thrash 'im like this." And she let fly—but unfortunately she 'it the pot of 'oney over the bed. The pot banged against the wall and crashed down in pieces and the lovely 'oney flowed out across the floor.

"Well, there goes the goose and the little gosling," said 'Arry, "and don't need fussing around with after all. Still—there's one good thing and that is that the pot didn't fall on me 'ead. It seems to me we've every reason to be 'appy with what's 'appened." And as 'e noticed that there was still some 'oney in one of the broken bits of pot 'e reached down for it and said with much satisfaction, "Well, missus, we'll just 'ave a taste of what's left and then after such a fright we'd better 'ave a bit of rest. After all, what does it matter if we get up a bit later than usual, the day'll still be long enough."

"You're right," said Trina, "there's always time enough. Did you 'ear about the snail as was once asked to a wedding? 'E set off all right, but didn't get there till they christened the first child. Even then 'e tripped over the fence in front of the 'ouse and said to 'imself, 'There you are—more 'aste, less speed'."

89

Lazy 'Arry; Sunny Jim; and Skinny Lizzie: Three Stories

Now when Lazy 'Arry mentioned the young feller and the cow and the blackbirds, 'e was really talking about a story that tells 'ow very fortunate those gents must be who've got clever servants on the manor who listen to everything they're told—and then go away and don't do it because they'd sooner follow their own bright ideas.

Once upon a time there was one such Sunny Jim who was sent out by 'is master to look for a strayed cow. 'E was gone a long while and the master thought to 'imself, "Ah, honest Jim, 'e don't spare 'imself any pains to do the job properly." But when the bloke never turned up, 'is master began to worry that something 'ad 'appened to 'im—so 'e upped and orfed to 'ave a look round for 'imself. Well—'e 'ad to look for a long time, but eventually 'e spotted the bloke a good way orf, running up and down in a field.

"Now then, Jim," says the master when 'e comes up with 'im, "'ave you found that cow that I sent you after?"

"No, master," says Jim, "I've not found the cow—but then I've not looked for it."

"Well, what 'ave you looked for, Jim?"

"Something a lot better—and what's more I've been lucky enough to find it."

"Well, what is it, Jim?"

"Three blackbirds,," says Jim.

"And where are they?" says the master.

"I'm looking at one, I'm listening to another, and I'm chasing the third," says the clever young feller.

So there you see the way of it: don't you worry about your guvnors and what they tell you to do. Much better follow your own ideas for what seems good at the time—then you'll be just as clever as Sunny Jim.

Now let's 'ear about Skinny Lizzie who fancied 'erself a good deal better than Lazy 'Arry and Fat Trina, who never let anything stir 'em out of their slumbers. For Skinny Lizzie burned 'erself up from morning till night and piled up so much work for 'er old man, Lanky Larry, that 'e 'ad more to carry than a donkey with three sacks full. But it was all to no purpose. They 'ad nothing and they got nothing.

Lazy 'Arry and friends

Now one evening, as Skinny Lizzie lay in bed, scarce able to lift 'er little finger for weariness, she was letting 'er thoughts keep going. Suddenly she shoved 'er old man in the ribs with 'er elbow and said, "Look 'ere, Larry, what I've been thinking. If I were to find a two-shilling piece, and someone were to give me a second one, then I'd borrow a third one and get you to give me a fourth. Then once we'd got the four two-shilling pieces together I'd go out and buy a little cow."

Well 'er old man thought that was a very bright idea. "I'm sure I don't know," said 'e, "where the two-bob bit's coming from that you want me to give you, but if you really do get all that money together and if you can buy a cow with it then you'll do well to get on with your plans." Then 'e added that 'e looked forward to this cow producing a calf so that 'e could refresh 'imself with a drink of milk whenever 'e felt like it.

"That milk's not for you," said 'is missus, "it's for the calf to suck so that it grows big and fat and we can sell it for a lot of money."

"Yes, indeed," said the man, "but—a little bit of milk—we could take a little bit of milk—that won't do any 'arm."

"And who's taught you what goes on with cows?" said 'is old woman, "whether it does 'arm, or whether it don't do 'arm, I won't 'ave it! And even if you stand on your 'ead, you're not getting a single drop of that milk! You great Lanky Larry! Just because you're never full do you think you're going to waste what I've got with so much trouble?"

"Woman," said Lanky Larry, "shut up or I'll smack you in the chops!"

"What," she shouted, "are you threatening me you great hunk, you great guts, you lazy 'Arry." And she set about tearing at 'is 'air, but Lanky Larry sat up in bed, grabbed 'er skinny arms in one 'and shoved 'er 'ead in the pillow with the other, and let her rage and swear until she fell asleep for weariness. But if, when they woke up next morning, they went on wrangling, or if they went out to look for the two-bob bits they wanted, I really don't know.

The Moon

A good time back there were a land where 'twas always pitch dark by night and the sky spread over all like coffin drapes—never a moon there to rise or set and never the chink of a star in the black darkness. At time o' the creation there'd just not been enough night-light to go round.

Well now—once upon a time four fellers set out from this land a-journeying and came to another country, where, come evening, and the sun down behind the hills, a glittering ball was there, standing in an oak-tree and sending out a soft, mellow light far and wide. You could see well enough by it to make out what was what even though 'tweren't so gaudy as the sun.

So these fellers stood there and asked an old farmer going by in his wagon what manner of light was this.

"That be the moon," says he. "Our old mayor come by 'im for a groat and fix 'im up there in the oak-tree. Now 'e's to souse 'im in oil every day and keep him clean so that 'e always burn bright. We do give 'im a groat a week for doing it."

When the farmer had drove on one of these chaps said, "We could put this here lamp to use—we've got an oak-tree to home as big as this 'un. We can hang it up there. Won't it be grand for us not to have to grope and grovel around in the dark every night!"

"I'll tell you what," said the second. "We'll fetch cart and horses and take this old moon off with us. The folks here can buy 'emselves another."

"I'm one for climbing trees," said the third, "I'll fetch 'en down soon enough." And the fourth brought up a cart and horses while number three climbed up the oak, drilled a hole in the moon, passed a rope through it and lowered it down.

Once the glittering ball was in the cart, they covered it over with a cloth so that no one would mark the robbery. Then they brought it cheerily back to their own land and set it up in a tall oak-tree. The old gaffers were cock-a-hoop, and the young folks likewise, when the new lamp posted its beams across all the fields lighting up rooms and bed-chambers everywhere. The dwarfs came out of their hidey-holes in the rocks and the piskies danced ring-dance in the meadows wearing their little red smocks.

The four fellers tended the moon with oil, trimmed his wick, and drew their weekly groat for wages. But they grew to be old gaffers themselves and when the first of 'em took sick and saw death was ready for him he willed for a quarter part of the moon to be put beside him in the grave as his portion. So when he was dead the mayor climbed up the tree, cut off a quarter with his hedging-shears and laid it in 'is coffin. The light of the moon dropped off a bit, but not so anyone noticed. Then, when the second died, he got the second quarter and the light dropped off a bit more. It got even less on the death of number three, who likewise took his portion, and by the time the fourth was buried the black darkness was back. When folks went out of an evening without a lantern they were always running their heads into one another.

Ah—but when those old bits of moon came together down below, where there'd never been aught but darkness—ah!—the dead grew all unpeaceable and woke up out their sleep. They were mazed to be able to see again (for the moonlight were quite enough for 'em, what with their eyes having got so weak—they'd never have borne the light of day).

Fetching down the moon

They all got up, cheerful as a parcel of sparrows, and took up living where they'd left off. One lot went gaming and dancing, others ran off to the ale-houses where they called for liquor, got themselves drunk, staggered and rolled about the place and, to finish up, took their cudgels and laid about themselves. The racket got worse by the minute and at last reached heaven itself.

St Peter—keeping the gate—reckoned it to be revolution in Hell and sent for the army of angels to chase back the Devil should he and his fellows be after storming the Halls of the Blest. But since they never came he climbed on his horse and rode off through the gate down to the underworld. There he settled all the dead back down again and told 'em to lie in their graves; then he took the moon back with him and hung it up in Heaven, and that's where it's been ever since.

Godfather Death

There was once a poor man who had twelve children, and he had to work day and night to find them enough to eat. When eventually the thirteenth arrived he nearly went off his head with despair. He rushed on to the high road, all set to ask the first person that he met to stand godfather at the child's christening.

Well, the first person turned out to be the Lord God himself. He already knew what the poor fellow's trouble was and said to him, "Ah, my poor friend, I am truly sorry for you. I will be the one to take your child from the font, and I will care for it and make it happy here on earth."

Then the man said, "Who are you?"

"I am the Lord God."

"Then I don't want you for a godfather," said the man, "you hand out everything to the rich and let the poor go hungry." (The man said that because he didn't know how wisely God disposes poverty and riches.) So he turned his back on the Lord and went on further.

Then the Devil came up to him and said, "What are you after? If you

want me to stand godfather to your child then you can be sure that I'll give him barrels and buckets of gold and all the pleasures of the world besides."

Then the man asked, "Who are you?"

"I am the Devil."

"Then I don't want you for a godfather," said the man. "You're forever doing folks harm and leading them astray." And he went on further.

Then Spindleshanks Death came up to him and said, "Let me stand godfather."

And the man asked, "Who are you?"

"I am Death the Leveller."

Then the man said, "You're the one. You take the rich and the poor alike. You're the man to be godfather."

And Death answered, "I will make your child rich and famous, for those who have me for a friend want for nothing."

Then the man said, "Well, next Sunday's the day of the christening. Be sure to be there at the right time." And, indeed, Death appeared just as he'd promised and stood godfather on his very best behaviour.

One day, after the boy had come of age, his godfather came up to him and said that the two of them should go along together. And he took him off into a wood and showed him a herb that grew there and said, "Now you shall have your godfather's present. I shall make you a famous physician. Whenever you are called to anyone sick I shall always appear to you, and if I stand at the sick man's head then you can speak up and say that you'd like to make him well again—and if you give him some of that plant then he'll recover. But if I stand at the sick man's feet, then he's mine and you must say that all help is in vain, and no physician in the world can save him. But take care that you don't use the plant against my will, for that will be the worse for you."

Well it didn't take long for the young man to become the most famous physician in the whole world. Everybody said: he needs only to look at you if you're sick and he knows at once how things are, whether you'll get better or whether you're going to die; and people came from far and wide, taking him to visit the sick, and giving him so much gold that he soon became a very rich man.

Now it so happened that the king of that land fell ill. The doctor was called and had to say what were the chances of recovery. But when he stepped up to the bedside, there was Death standing at the sick man's feet and no plant of any kind likely to do any good at all.

"Ah! but what if I could trick him for once," thought the doctor. "For sure he's not going to like it, but after all I am his godchild and he might wink an eye for once in a while; let's take the risk." And he seized hold of the sick man and laid him round the other way so that Death was now standing at his head. Then he gave him some of the plant and the king recovered and became fit and well again.

But Death came to the doctor with a face all dark with anger, and he threatened him with his finger and said, "You have made a fool out of me. This time though I'll forget it, because you are my godchild. But if you dare to do it again it will be all your life's worth. I will take you off myself."

Soon after this the king's daughter fell desperately ill. She was his only child and he wept for her day and night till he was almost blind, and he let it be known that whoever could save her from death should marry her and inherit the crown. Well, when our doctor came to the sick girl's bedside he saw Death standing there at her feet. Straight away he should have remembered his godfather's warning, but he was so crazed by her beauty and by the joy of being her husband that he cast all good sense to the winds. He didn't see Death's angry look or how he raised up his hand and threatened him with his bony fist; he lifted up the sick girl and laid her head there where her feet had been. Then he gave her the herb and at once her cheeks grew red and life stirred again within her.

Twice now cheated of his rightful dues, Death strode up to the doctor on his long legs and said, "Now it's all up with you; now it's your turn," and he grasped the doctor with his icy hand so hard that he could do nothing about it, and he led him to an underground cave. Here he saw thousands upon thousands of lights burning in uncountable rows— some big, some not so big, and others small. At every moment some were extinguished, while others burned up again, so that the little flames seemed to dance hither and thither in a continuously changing pattern.

"Look here," said Death, "these are the lights of men's lives. The big ones belong to children, the less big ones to married people in their best years, and the small ones belong to the aged. But even children and young people may often have only a little flame."

"Show me the light of my life," said the doctor, with the idea that it would still be pretty tall. And Death pointed to a tiny candle-end, which was even then threatening to go out, and said, "There, that's the one."

"But Godfather, dear, kind Godfather," said the frightened doctor, "light me a new one. Please, for my sake, light one so that I can enjoy my life, so that I can be king and marry the beautiful princess."

"I cannot do it," said Death. "one light must go out before ever another is lit."

"Well then, put the old one on top of a new one so that it will start to burn when the other is finished," pleaded the doctor. And Death moved as though to do what he wanted, fetching along a big, clear light, but because he still wished to have his revenge he purposely fumbled the change and the little candle-end fell over and went out. Straight away the doctor sank to the ground and so himself came into the hands of his Godfather Death.

The Fisherman and His Wife

Once, a while back, there was a fisherman who lived with his old woman in a piss-pot down by the sea; and the fisherman went off every day and fished. And he fished and he fished. He'd sit there with his line, looking down through the clear water. And he sat and he sat.

Well, one day his line got pulled down, deep under, and when he hauled it up he hauled up a huge flounder as well. Then the flounder said to him, "Wait on, fisherman, let me alone; truth is, I'm not really a flounder but an enchanted prince. What good'll it do you to kill me? I'll not taste very nice. Put me back in the water and let me swim."

"All right," said the man, "you needn't take on so. You can be sure I'll let swim a flounder that talks." And with that he puts him back into the clear water, and the flounder swims to the bottom, leaving a long streak of blood behind him. The fisherman gets up and goes back to his old woman in the piss-pot.

"Well, man," says his old woman, "haven't you caught anything today?"

"Nay," says the man, "I caught a flounder that said he were an enchanted prince, but I let him go back again."

"D'you mean to say you didn't wish for anything?" says his old woman.

"Nay," says the man, "what should I wish for?"

"Eee!" says his old woman, "look at us, stuck here forever in this stinking piss-pot. You might have wished a little cottage for us. Go on back down there and call him; tell him we'd like to have a little cottage. He'd surely give us that."

"Aw," says the man. "D'you want me to go back there again."

"Ay," says his old woman, "you caught him, and you kindly let him go again; he'll surely give us that. Go on, be off with you."

Well, the man didn't think that was altogether proper, but then he didn't know how to stand up to his old woman, so he went back down to the sea again.

When he got there the sea was all green and yellow—not clear like it had been before. So he stood there and said:

> "Mannikin, mannikin, timpe tee
> Flounder, flounder in the sea
> My old missis Ilsebill
> Will not have it as I will."

Then the flounder came swimming up and said, "Nah, what d'you want then?"

"Aw," said the man, "you know as how I caught you. Well my old woman says I should have asked for a wish. She doesn't want to go on living in the piss-pot, she'd like to have a little cottage."

"Go on home, man," said the flounder, "she's got it all." Then the man went home and his old woman wasn't sitting in the piss-pot any more, for there was a little cottage with his missis sitting by the door on a bench.

Then she took him by the hand and said to him, "Come in here, man—just see this; it's a good sight better." And they went in and there in the cottage was a little hall and a pretty little parlour and a bedroom, with a bed for each of them, and a kitchen and a dining-room; all done out with the best furniture and fitted with the best in pots and pans, tin-ware, copper-ware, whatever you can think of. And at the back there was a little yard with chickens and ducks, and a little garden with fruit trees and vegetables.

"Just see," said the wife, "isn't that lovely?"

"Yes," said the man, "that's the way it ought to be; now we shall be very comfy."

"We'll have to think about that," said his old woman, and with that they had a bite of supper and went to bed.

Well, everything went along gradely for a couple of weeks, then the old woman said, "Look here, man, this cottage is altogether too poky and the garden's too small; your flounder could easily have given us a bigger place. I wouldn't mind at all living in a great stone castle. Go on down to the flounder, let him give us a castle."

"Aw, missis," said the man, "this cottage is good enough for us; what would we do with a castle?"

"That's what I want," said his old woman, "go on with you, the flounder can always do things like that."

"Nay, missis," said the man, "the flounder's only just given us the cottage. I can't rightly go to him again, he might not like it."

"Go on," said the old woman, "he can do it, and he'll like to do it. Be off with you."

"The man's heart was heavy, and he didn't want to go. He said to himself, "It's just not right." But off he went.

When he came to the sea, the water was all blue and violet, grey and thick, not green and yellow, but it was still calm. So he stood there and said:

> "Mannikin, mannikin, timpe tee
> Flounder, flounder in the sea
> My old missis Ilsebill
> Will not have it as I will."

"Nah, what d'you want then?" said the flounder.

"Aw," said the man all embarrassed-like, "she wants to live in a great stone castle."

"Go on home, man," said the flounder, "she's by the front-door."

Then the man went home, thinking he'd come to the house, but when he got there what should he find but a great stone palace, with his old woman up the top of the steps all ready to go in.

Then she took him by the hand and said, "Come in here, man", and at that he went in with her; and in the castle there was a great hall with a marble floor, and there were crowds of servants throwing open doors all over the place. The walls were all shining, with tapestries hanging on them, and the rooms were full of tables and chairs—all pure gold—and there were crystal chandeliers hanging from the ceiling and all the rooms and chambers were covered with carpets. There was food and the very best wine on the tables, so that they could eat and drink when they pleased, while behind the house there was a great courtyard with stables and cowsheds and the very best in coaches and carriages. There was a great big beautiful garden too, with the loveliest flowers and great trees, and there was a park, more than half a mile long, with stags in it and deer and rabbits and everything you could ask for.

"Ee," said the old woman, "isn't that lovely?"

"Aw, yes," said the man, "that's the way it ought to be; now we shall be able to live in this castle all very nicely."

"We'll have to think about that," said his old woman, "we'll sleep on it." And with that they went to bed.

The next morning the old woman was the first to wake up. It was just first light and she could see from her bed all the beautiful countryside lying in front of her. Her man was still snoring, so she dug him in the ribs with her elbow and said, "Here, man, get up and take a look out of that window. Why can't we be king over all that country? Go on down to the flounder and say we want to be king."

"Aw, missis," said the man, "who wants to be king? I don't want to be king."

"Nah," said his old woman, "if you don't want to be king, then I'll be king. Get on down to the flounder and tell him I want to be king."

"Aw, missis," said the man, "what do you want to be king for? I can't say that to him."

"Why ever not?" said his old woman. "You be off with you. I must be king and that's that."

So the man went down all shamed over his wife wanting to be king. "That's not right, that's just not right," he said to himself. He didn't want to go, but off he went.

And when he came to the sea, the sea was all black and grey and the water was all seething and stank real foul. So he stood there and said:

> "Mannikin, mannikin, timpe tee
> Flounder, flounder in the sea
> My old missis Ilsebill
> Will not have it as I will."

"Well, what does she want now?" said the flounder.

"Aw," said the man, "she wants to be king."

"Go on home," said the flounder, "she's got it all."

Then the man went home, and as he came up to the palace he saw that the castle had got much bigger, with a great tower covered in carvings; and the sentries stood at the door and there were crowds of soldiers with drums and trumpets. And when he came into the house everything was pure marble and gold, with silk hangings and great golden tassles. Then the doors of the great hall opened up, with all the court there, and his old woman was sitting on a great high throne made of gold and diamonds, and she had on a great golden crown and carried a sceptre of pure gold and precious stones, and on either side of her there stood six young lasses in a row, each one taller by a head than the one next door.

Then he stood in front of her and said, "Well, missis, so now you're king." And he stood there and looked at her and after he'd looked for a bit he said, "Aw, missis, this is all very nice now you're king; now we don't have to wish for anything else."

"Nay, man," said his old woman, shifting about on her seat, "it's very tedious and boring up here; I can't bear it any longer. Go on down to the flounder, tell him I'm king and now I want to be emperor as well."

"Aw missis," said the man, "what do you want to be emperor for?"

"Man," said she, "get off to the flounder; I must be emperor and that's that."

"Aw, missis," said the man, "he can't make you emperor; I can't say that to the flounder; there's nobbut one emperor in the country;

emperor's not for flounders to make; he just can't do it."

"Wait on," said his old woman, "if I'm king then you're my man; you must be off at once. Go on, get off with you. He can make kings, so he can make emperors as well. I must and will be emperor, so you go and see about it." So he had to go. But as he went along he felt very scared, and as he walked he said to himself, "That's not good at all—emperor's too brazen—the flounder 'll be done with us all this time."

Then he came to the sea and the sea was still all black and thick and beginning to boil up in itself so that it came foaming in, and it flew about so in the bitter wind that it curdled and the man was right terrified. So he stood there and said:

> "Mannikin, mannikin, timpe tee
> Flounder, flounder in the sea
> My old missis Ilsebill
> Will not have it as I will."

"What does she want now?" said the flounder.

"Aw, flounder," said he, "my old woman wants to be emperor."

"Go on home," said the flounder, "she's got it all."

Then the man went home, and when he got there he found the whole castle turned into polished marble with alabaster statues and golden decorations. The soldiers were marching up and down in front of the door, blowing trumpets and banging side-drums and kettle-drums, while inside you could see barons and counts and dukes walking about as servants; and they opened up the doors for him and these doors were all made of pure gold. And as he came in there he saw his old woman, sitting up on a throne, two miles high and made out of a single piece of gold; and she was wearing a great golden crown which was six feet high, all set about with diamonds and rubies. In one hand she had the sceptre and in the other the great orb of state, and on both sides of her were standing her gentlemen-at-arms in two lines with each man a little shorter than the man next door, so that at one end there were great giants of fellows two miles high and at the other little tiny dwarfs who weren't even so big as my little finger. In front of them there were standing a whole lot of dukes and princes.

So the man went up among them all and said, "Well, missis, so you're emperor now?"

"Yes," said she, "I'm emperor."

Then he went and stood and looked at her straight, and after he'd looked for a bit, he said, "Well, missis, this is all very nice now you're emperor."

"Man," said she, "what are you standing there for? Now I'm emperor I want to be pope as well. Go on down to the flounder."

"Aw, woman," said the man, "what will you be thinking of next? You can't be pope. There's only one pope in Christendom; he can't make you that."

"Man," said she, "I will be pope. Get off with you straight away. I must be pope."

"Nay, woman," said the man, "I can't say that to him; that's not good at all; that's too big; the flounder can't make you into a pope."

"Don't talk nonsense, man," said the old woman, "if he can make emperors he can make popes too. Get off with you. If I'm emperor then you're my man; will you go on now?"

Then he was proper scared, and he went off trembling and shaking, and his knees were banging together and his legs felt like jelly. And a great wind blew over the land, and clouds flew across and everything got dim as though night was coming on. Leaves fell from the trees and the water boiled like someone was cooking, and it seethed up the bank; and far away he could see ships in trouble, tossing about on the waves. But there was still a bit of blue in the middle of the sky, even though all round the edges it was red with the makings of a terrible storm. Then he went and stood there half out of his wits with fright and said:

> "Mannikin, mannikin, timpe tee
> Flounder, flounder in the sea
> My old missis Ilsebill
> Will not have it as I will."

"Well, what does she want now?" said the flounder.

"Aw," said the man, "she wants to be pope."

"Go on home," said the flounder, "she's got it all."

Then he went home, and when he got there, he found it was a kind of great church with lots of palaces all round it. He shoved his way through all the folk that were there, and inside he saw it was all lit up with thousands and thousands of candles, and his old woman was dressed in pure gold, sitting up there on a much higher throne with three great golden crowns on her head. And round her there were so many holy people, and up both sides in front of her there were two lines of candles, with the biggest as thick and fat as the biggest tower you can think of, down to the smallest like a candle on a cake, and all the emperors and kings were kneeling there kissing her slippers.

"Well, woman," he said, and gave her a straight look, "so you're pope now?"

"Yes," said she, "I'm pope." Then he went and stood and looked at her, and it were as though he were looking at the bright sun.

After he'd looked for a bit, he said, "Aw, missis, this is all very nice now you're pope!" But she stayed looking stiff as a tree and never stretched nor stirred herself at all.

Then he said, "Now, missis, let it be now you're pope. You can't want aught else."

"I shall have to think about that," said his old woman, and with that they both went to bed. But she couldn't let it be, and she was that greedy she couldn't sleep for thinking what else she might become.

The man slept right good and sound, because of all the walking he'd done that day, but his old woman tossed and turned from one side of the bed to the other all the night long, thinking what she might become, and she couldn't think of anything.

By-and-by though, the sun began to rise, and when she saw the dawn breaking she sat herself up in bed, looked around, and when she saw through the window how the sun was coming up, she said to herself, "Ha! couldn't I make the sun and moon rise?—Man!" she said, digging him in the ribs with her elbow, "man, wake up; go on down to the flounder and tell him I want to be the good Lord himself."

Now the man was still hardly awake, but he was so frightened when he heard this that he fell out of bed. He didn't think to have heard aright, and he rubbed his eyes and said, "Aw, missis, what's that you said?"

"Man," she said, "if I can't make the sun and moon to rise, if I've just got to sit here watching while the sun and moon come up, then I can't do with it. I shan't have a moment's peace till I can make them come up myself." Then she looked at him right sharpish so that he couldn't help but tremble. "Get off with you at once; I want to be the good Lord himself."

"Aw, missis," said the man, and he got down on his knees, "the flounder can't do that. Mebbe he can make emperors and popes, but leave it at that; please, just stay pope."

Then she got wicked angry. Her hair stood up all round her head and she shrieked out, "I can't do with it. I can't do with this a minute longer. You get off with yourself!" So he pulled on his britches and dashed off like he was mad.

But the storm was raging something terrible and blowing so he could scarcely stand on his two feet. Trees and houses were tumbling down, the hills were shaking and bits of rock were crashing into the sea. The heavens were black as pitch; there was thunder and lightning, and the sea hurled up waves as high as steeples and mountains, all crowned with caps of white foam. So he called—and could never hear his own words:

> "Mannikin, mannikin, timpe tee
> Flounder, flounder in the sea
> My old missis Ilsebill
> Will not have it as I will."

"Well, what does she want now?" said the flounder.
"Aw," said he, "she wants to be like the good Lord himself."
"Go on home," said the flounder, "she's sitting in the piss-pot again."
And there they stayed sitting until this very day.

The fisherman goes to do the bidding of his wife

The Twelve Dancing Princesses
or, The Shoes That Were Danced to Pieces

Once upon a time there was a king, and he had twelve daughters, each more beautiful than the last. They all slept together in one room and every night, as soon as they were ready for bed, the king would see to it that their door was shut fast and bolted. But in the morning, when he opened it up again, he'd see that the slippers by their beds were all danced to pieces, and no one could tell how that had happened.

So the king gave out that if anyone could discover where they went off to in the night, he should have the princess of his choice for his wife and would be king afterwards. But if anyone who made the attempt had, after three days and three nights, found out nothing, he should forfeit his life.

It wasn't long before a king's son was so bold as to make the attempt. He was given a good welcome and, in the evening, taken to the room next door to the princesses' bed-chamber. They set up a bed for him there and he was left to keep a look-out for where the princesses went off to and danced. And so that they couldn't get up to anything in secret or take themselves off to some other place, the doors between the two rooms were left open.

It wasn't long, though, before the young prince grew all heavy-eyed and fell asleep, and, in the morning, when he woke up, he found that the twelve had been off to the dance, for their slippers were there with the soles worn through to nothing. The same thing happened on the second and third evenings and the king's son was taken off and beheaded without more ado; and from that time on many more came to take up the challenge but they all paid for it with their lives.

Now it so happened that there was a poor soldier who'd been badly wounded and couldn't serve any more with the colours. He found himself on the road to the city where this king lived and on the way he met an old woman who asked him where he was off to.

"Not something I rightly know myself," he answered, and added by way of a joke, "but I wouldn't mind finding out where those princesses dance away their shoes, so that I could get to be king."

"Well that's not so hard," said the old woman, "you must be sure not to drink the wine they bring you in the evening and then you must make out that you're fast asleep," and she gave him a little cloak saying that when he put it on he'd be invisible and would find it easy enough to creep after the twelve princesses.

The soldier took all this good advice, plucked up his courage, and went before the king as suitor to the twelve princesses. He was well received like all the others and was dressed up in a right royal suit of clothes. Then in the evening, when it was time to go to bed he was taken to the side-room and the eldest of the princesses brought him a cup of wine; but the soldier had tied a sponge under his chin and he let all the wine run down into that, drinking never a drop. Then he laid himself down and, after a while, began to snore as though he'd never wake again.

When the twelve princesses heard that, they laughed and the eldest said: here was another who might have saved his skin. Then they got up, opened their cupboards and their closets and their drawers, and brought out some magnificent dresses. They tricked themselves out in

front of their mirrors and jumped about the room in anticipation of the coming dance. Only the youngest said, "I don't know—it's all very well—you're all enjoying yourselves, but I've got a strange feeling that something's going to go wrong."

"You're just a silly goose who's afraid of everything," said the eldest princess. "Have you forgotten how many kings' sons have come to us all in vain? As for this soldier, even if I hadn't brought him a sleepy-drink the old fellow would be dead to the world."

When they were all ready, they took a good look at the soldier, but he had his eyes well closed and never moved a muscle, so that they thought themselves quite safe. Then the eldest went to her bed, banged on it, and at once it sank into the ground and they all went down through the opening, one after another, with the eldest in front.

The soldier, who had watched everything, didn't lose any time. He put on the little cloak and set off down behind the youngest princess. Half way down the staircase, though, he stepped on the hem of her dress and frightened her so that she cried out, "Who's that? Who's holding on to my dress?"

"Oh, don't be such a simpleton," said the eldest. "You've caught yourself on a nail."

So they went on down to the bottom of the staircase, and when they were there they found themselves in a magnificent avenue of trees where all the leaves were of silver, glittering and glinting. The soldier thought he'd better get himself proof of this, so he broke off one of the branches and at once there was a loud cracking from the tree.

Again the youngest princess cried, "It's not all right! What about that noise?"

But the eldest said, "That's our princes. They're shooting off guns for joy because we've released them."

Then they came to an avenue of trees where all the leaves were of gold, and then to a third where they were of pure diamond, and in both of these the soldier broke off a branch so that each time there was a loud crack and each time the youngest almost collapsed from fright. But the eldest kept saying it was only the princes shooting for joy.

They kept on going till at last they came to a wide stretch of water,

Twelve princesses are taken to the dance

where twelve little boats were waiting for them, and in each boat a handsome prince. The princesses got in, one to a boat, and the soldier got in with the youngest. Then the prince said, "I don't know—the boat seems a lot heavier today. I've got to row with all my strength just to keep it moving."

"That must be because of the warm weather," said the princess. "It seems very hot to me as well."

Now on the far side of the water there stood a splendid, brightly lit castle resounding with the gay music of drums and trumpets. They rowed up to it, went in, and each prince danced with his own princess. As for the soldier, he danced too—invisible though he was—and whenever a princess took a glass of wine, he would drink it up, so that the glass was empty before she could try it. This was something else that worried the youngest, but the eldest always persuaded her to keep quiet.

They stayed there dancing till three o'clock in the morning, by which time their slippers were quite danced to pieces and they all had to stop. The princes rowed them back across the water, but this time the soldier sat in the bow of the eldest princess' boat.

On reaching the shore, they all said farewell to their princes and promised to come again on the following night; then, when they had got to the staircase, the soldier ran ahead and jumped into his bed, so that when the twelve came slowly and wearily limping up the stairs, he was once again snoring so noisily that they could all hear him, and they told themselves, "We're safe enough from him." Then they took off their beautiful dresses, laid them away, placed their raggedy slippers under the beds and settled down to sleep.

The next morning the soldier had nothing to say, wishing only to see these strange events again and he went with the twelve princesses on the second and third nights. Everything took place just as it had done the first time, with the slippers being danced to pieces just as before. On the third visit, though, the soldier took for a token one of the drinking-glasses.

When the time arrived for him to give some account of himself, he tucked away the three branches and the glass and came before the king, while the twelve princesses stood behind the door to hear what he had to say. When the king put the question, "Where have my twelve daughters been off to in the night, wearing out their slippers?" the soldier answered, "With twelve princes in an underground castle," and he explained how it was and brought out his tokens.

Then the king sent for his daughters and asked them if the soldier's words were true, and, since they saw that they were discovered and that lying would do no good, they confessed everything. At this the king asked the soldier which of them he would have for his wife, and the soldier answered, "I'm not so young any more; give me the eldest." And so, on the self-same day, the wedding was held and the soldier was pronounced heir to the kingdom.

As for the princes, they remained enchanted for as many days more as the nights that they'd spent dancing with the twelve princesses.

King Throstlebeard

A king had a daughter, beautiful beyond all telling, but so proud and haughty with it that no suitor was good enough for her. She turned down one after another and, what's more, made fun of them as well. So—one day the king had a great feast prepared and invited to it from near and far all the men who wanted to marry his daughter. They were all lined up in a row, according to their rank and dignity—kings first, then dukes, then counts, then barons and last of all knights of the realm. Then the princess was led down the row, but she took exception to every one of them. One was too fat for her: "Barrelguts," said she; another too tall: "Tall and skinny, walks like a ninny"; a third was too short: "Short and stocky, never lucky"; a fourth too pale: "Death warmed up"; a fifth too red: "Gobble, gobble turkey-cock"; and a sixth not straight enough: "Greenstick dried behind the stove"—and so she went on finding fault with each of them.

But she had particular fun at the expense of a kindly young king at the head of the procession whose chin had grown a bit crooked. "Hey, hey, hey," she called, laughing all the time, "he's got a chin like a throstle's beak," and from that time on he came to be known as "Throstlebeard".

As for the old king, however, when he saw his daughter do nothing but mock everyone and put to shame all the suitors who'd gathered there, he was filled with rage and swore she'd have for husband the firstmost beggar that came to his door.

A few days later a wandering minstrel started singing under the window, hoping to pick up a few alms. When the king heard him he said, "Let him come up"—and the minstrel was brought in in his dirty, ragged clothes, and he sang in front of the king and the princess, and, when he'd finished, asked for his reward. Then the king said, "Your singing has pleased me so much, that I shall give you my daughter there to be your wife." The princess was horrified, but the king said, "I swore an oath to give you to the firstmost beggarman and that will I do." Pleading was useless. The priest was fetched and without more ado she was married to the minstrel.

When that was over the king said, "Now it's not suitable for beggarmaids to stay in my castle; you and your man can be off together."

The beggarman led her out by the hand and she had to go with him on the path he took. When they came to a great wood she asked,

"And whose are all these mighty woods?"

"His Majesty King Throstlebeard's—
   If you'd taken him they would be yours."

"O what a foolish finnicky maid,
   Not to have had King Throstlebeard."

Then they came to a meadow and she asked again,

"And whose are all these lovely fields?"

"His Majesty King Throstlebeard's—
   If you'd taken him they would be yours."

"O what a foolish, finnicky maid,
   Not to have had King Throstlebeard."

Then they came to a great city and she asked again,

"And whose are all these squares and streets?"

"His Majesty King Throstlebeard's—
  If you'd taken him they would be yours."

"O what a foolish, finnicky maid,
  Not to have had King Throstlebeard."

"I don't like it at all," said the minstrel, "hearing you wish you had another man for husband. Aren't I good enough for you?" And at last they came to a little old cottage, and she said,

"Ah God! Look at that for a dingy house.
  Whoever could live in such a mingy house."

And the minstrel answered, "That's my house and your house, and that's where we shall live together."

She had to bend down to get in through the low doorway, and—"Where are the servants?" said the princess.

"What servants?" answered the minstrel. "What you want done you must do yourself—but just now light the fire and put on a pot to boil for supper. I'm tired out."

But the princess knew nothing of lighting fires or cooking suppers, and the beggarman had to set to with his own hands to make something of it all. When they'd eaten their poor rations they went to bed, but, come the morning, he drove her out early to clean up the house.

For a few days they lived like this, plain and simple, eating up what was in the larder.

Then the man said, "Woman, we're not going on much longer eating without earning. You'll have to weave some baskets." He went out, cut some withies and brought them home—then she began weaving them, but the stiff withies cut up her tender hands.

"I can see that's no good," said the man. "Rather try spinning, perhaps you're better at that." She sat down and set about spinning, but the tough threads soon cut into her soft fingers so that the blood ran down.

"Well see here," said the man. "You're good for no work and I've got a bad bargain with you. Still—I'll try and start a trade in pots and crocks: you can find a place for yourself in the market and sell the stuff."

"Alas!" she thought, "what if people from my father's country come and see me sitting in the market crying pots and pans, how they'll mock me!" But it did no good; she had to give in if she didn't want to die of hunger.

The first day things went well—people were glad to buy the lady's goods because she was so beautiful, and they paid what she asked (indeed many gave her the money and left her with the pots as well). So now they lived off what she earned for as long as it lasted, then the man laid in a fresh stock of new crockery. She sat down with it in a corner of the market-place and set it out round her and cried her wares. But suddenly a great drunken hussar came galloping by and rode straight over the pots so that they were all shattered in a thousand pieces. She started to cry and was too scared to think what she should do.

"Alas! what will become of me," she said. "What will my man have to say about this!" and she ran home and told him of her misfortune.

"Well who on earth goes and sits in a corner of the market to sell crockery?" said the man. "Give over crying, I can see well enough you're no use in any steady job. I've just been up at our king's castle and I asked them if they weren't able to use a kitchen-maid. They've promised me they'll take you on—and you'll get free grub out of it."

So the king's daughter became a kitchen-maid, and always had to be on hand for the cook and do the nastiest work. She fastened a little jar in both her pockets so that she could take back home her share of the left-overs and they lived off this.

Now it so happened that the wedding of the king's eldest son was to be celebrated and the poor woman went upstairs and stood by the door of the room to watch. And when the candles were all lit and the guests came in, each one more beautiful than the last, and everything so full of splendour and magnificence, she thought of her own fate with a sad heart and cursed her pride and arrogance that had humbled her and cast her into such deep poverty. From time to time servants would throw her a few crumbs of the rare sweetmeats which were being carried in and out and whose smell caught in her nostrils, and these crumbs she would put in her jars to take home.

Suddenly the king's son came in, dressed in silk and satin, with a gold chain round his neck. And when he saw the beautiful woman standing in the doorway he seized her by the hand to dance with her, but she would not, and was horrified to see that it was King Throstlebeard, who had sought to marry her and whom she'd turned away in mockery. But her struggling was all to no good; he drew her into the room, and then— the band broke that held her pockets and the jars fell out so that the soup was spilled and the left-overs scattered. And when everyone saw that, there was a great shout of mocking laughter and she was so ashamed that she wished herself a thousand fathoms under the earth. She sprang out of the door and sought to flee, but a man caught her on the stairs and brought her back; and when she looked at him she saw once again that it was King Throstlebeard.

Kindly he said to her, "Don't be afraid. The minstrel, who lived with you in the dingy house, and I are one and the same person. I disguised myself for love of you—and indeed I was the hussar too, who galloped through your pots. It's all been done to bend your proud spirit and to punish you for your pride when you mocked me."

Then she wept bitter tears and said, "I have done a terrible wrong and am not fit to be your wife."

But he said, "Be comforted; the bad days are past and now we shall celebrate our wedding."

And the maids-in-waiting came and dressed her in splendid clothes, and her father came with all his court to wish her happiness at her wedding to King Throstlebeard, and now it was a time of rejoicing. What larks we'd have had if we'd been there too!

King Throstlebeard in disguise

Hansel and Gretel

On the edge of a great forest a poor woodcutter lived with his wife and his two children—the lad, Hansel, and the lass, Gretel. He'd little enough to put on their plates or into the pantry, so that, once when a great famine seized the land, there came a day when he could get nothing for them to eat at all.

Late on that evening, thinking to himself in bed, and tossing and turning with worry, he let out a great groan and said to his wife, "What's to become of us? How can we feed those poor kids when we've not even got enough for ourselves?"

"I'll tell you what, man," answered his wife, "tomorrow early we'll take them out into the thickest part of the forest. We'll light a fire for them and give them each a bit more bread. Then we'll get off to our work and leave them on their own. They'll never find their way back home again, so we'll be rid of them."

"Woman—no!" said the man. "I'll not do it. How could I have the heart to leave my children alone in the forest? The wild animals'd come soon enough and tear them to pieces."

"You damn fool!" said she. "That means that you'll have all four of us die of hunger—well, you'd better start planing up the boards for our coffins." And she left him no peace till he agreed.

"Even so," he said, "I'm grieving for those poor children."

Now the two children also hadn't been able to sleep for hunger and they'd heard everything their mother said to their father. Gretel cried bitterly and said to Hansel, "Now it's the end of us."

"Quiet, Gretel," said Hansel, "don't worry yourself. I'll find a way for us." And when his parents had gone to sleep, he got up, put on his jacket, opened up the lower bit of the door and crept out. The moon was shining brightly out there and the white pebbles that lay round the house glinted like brand-new silver shillings. Hansel bent down and stuck as many of them in his jacket pocket as would go.

Then he went back and said to Gretel, "Calm down, little sister, and go to sleep—God won't desert us," and he climbed back into his bed.

At break of day, before the sun had even had a chance to rise, the woman came and woke up the two children. "Get up you old lazybones, we want to be off to the forest to get wood." Then she gave each of them a little piece of bread, saying, "There now, that's something for your dinner, but don't eat it sooner, because you'll get no more." Gretel stowed the bread in her apron, because Hansel had his pockets full of stones. Then they all set out together down the path into the forest.

After they'd gone along for a while, Hansel stopped and peered back towards the house—not once, but time and again. "Hansel, what are you doing, gawping back there," said his father. "Watch out you don't lose the use of your legs."

"Ah, Papa," said Hansel, "I'm looking back at my little white cat who's sitting up there on the roof, saying good-bye to me."

"Idiot," said the woman, "that's not your cat, that's the first of the sun shining on the chimney." But Hansel hadn't been looking at his cat or anything else, but taking one of the white pebbles out of his pocket and putting it on the ground.

When they got to the middle of the forest the father said, "Right now, get some wood together you kids, and I'll make up a fire so's you don't freeze." So Hansel and Gretel collected up a pile of brushwood about as high as a small mountain, and this was lit; and when the flames were leaping up tall the woman said, "Now lie down beside the fire, you two, and have a rest. We're going into the forest to chop wood. When we've done we'll come back and fetch you."

Hansel and Gretel sat by the fire, and when midday came they ate their little bit of bread. And because they could hear the blows of an axe they thought their father wasn't far off. But it wasn't an axe at all; it was a branch that he'd tied to a dead tree that knocked against it in the wind. And after they'd sat there a good while their eyes closed from weariness and they fell fast asleep.

When they finally awoke it was already deep night. Gretel began to cry and said, "How are we ever to get out of this forest?"

But Hansel comforted her. "Just wait awhile till the moon's up then we'll soon find our way." And, sure enough, once the full moon had risen Hansel took his little sister by the hand and sought out those pebbles, all shining like brand-new silver shillings, which showed them the way.

All night long they walked and at daybreak they came again to their father's house. They knocked at the door and when the woman opened it and saw Hansel and Gretel standing there she said, "You wicked children, why did you stay sleeping so long in the forest? We thought you were never coming back." But their father rejoiced, because it had cut him to the heart that he'd left them behind all alone.

It wasn't long though before, once again, there was famine in every corner of the land and the children heard how the mother said to the father in bed at night, "Everything's been eaten up again. We've got just half a load of bread left over and when that's gone the kissing'll have to stop. The kids must be put out—we'll take them deeper into the forest so that they'll never find their way out again—otherwise we'll never save ourselves."

But this came hard on the man's heart and he thought, "It would be better for you to share your last crumbs with the children,"—but the woman wouldn't listen to anything he said, nagged him and reproached him. So it was a case of "Once you say 'A' you've got to say 'B'," and because he'd given in the first time, he had to give in the second too.

Once again, though, the children were still awake and listened to the whole conversation. So when the parents were asleep Hansel got up again and tried to go out to gather pebbles as before, but the woman had locked the door and he couldn't get out. But he comforted his little sister saying, "Don't cry, Gretel, and sleep well. God will help us."

Early the next morning the woman came and hauled the children out of bed. They were given their bit of bread (but it was smaller than the last time) and on the way Hansel crumbled it in his pocket and kept stopping to throw little crumbs to the ground. "Hansel, what are you standing around gawping at," said his father. "Get on with you."

"Oh! I'm looking back at my little dove, sitting up there on the roof, saying good-bye to me."

"Idiot!" said the woman, "that's not your little dove, that's the first of the sun shining on the chimney." But gradually Hansel threw all his crumbs of bread on to the path.

The woman led the children deeper and deeper into the forest to places they'd never been in their lives before. Once again a big fire was made and the mother said, "Stay sitting there, you children, and if you feel tired you can sleep for a bit. We're going into the forest to chop wood and this evening, when we've done, we'll come and fetch you."

Well—since it was midday, Gretel shared her bread with Hansel, who had, of course, scattered his bit back on the path. Then they fell asleep and the evening passed, but no one came for those poor children. They didn't wake till it was dark night and Hansel comforted his little sister and said, "Just wait, Gretel, till the moon comes up, then we'll see the little bits of bread I scattered and they'll show us the way back home." So when the moon rose they got up, but they found never a crumb of bread, because all the thousands of birds that fly around in the woods and fields had pecked them and eaten them.

"Never mind," said Hansel, "we'll soon find the way"—but they didn't find it. They walked the whole night long and then a whole day, morning till evening, but they couldn't come out of the forest, and they grew so hungry, for they had nothing to eat but a few berries which they found growing wild. And since they were so tired that their legs wouldn't carry them a step further, they lay down under a tree and slept.

So this was the third morning since they'd left their father's house.

They started to walk again but they wandered even deeper into the forest and if help hadn't come soon they must have pined away. But towards midday they saw a beautiful little bird, as white as snow, sitting on a branch, and it sang so sweetly that they stood still and listened to it. And when it had finished, it flapped its wings and flew off in front of them and they went after it till they came to a little house, where it settled down on the roof—and as they came close they saw that this little house was built of bread and roofed with cakes, and the windows were clear, transparent sugar.

"We'll set to there," said Hansel, "and for what we're about to receive may the Lord make us truly thankful. I'll eat a bit of the roof, Gretel, and you can try the windows—they look sweet enough." And Hansel reached up and broke himself off a piece of the roof to see how it tasted, while Gretel stood by the window-panes and nibbled at them. It was then that a little thin voice came out of the room:

"Nibble, nibble mousekin,
Who's nibbling at my housekin?"

and the children answered,

"The wind so wild,
The Heavenly Child"

and they went on eating without letting themselves be put off.

Hansel, who was really enjoying the roof, tore down a great piece of it, and Gretel pushed out a whole round window-pane and sat down and did herself well by it. Then the door suddenly opened and there came creeping out an ancient woman leaning on a crutch.

Hansel and Gretel were so scared that they let fall what they were holding; but the old woman shook her head and said, "Aiee, you dear little things, and who's brought you here? Why don't you come inside and rest here; no one's going to harm you," and she grasped both of them by the hand and led them into her little house. Then lots of food was brought in to them—milk and pancakes with sugar, apples and nuts. Afterwards two beautiful little beds were made up with white sheets, and Hansel and Gretel climbed in and thought they were in Heaven.

Hansel and Gretel at the house in the woods

But the old woman was only pretending to be friendly. She was really an evil witch, who lay in wait for children and had built the gingerbread house simply to entice them. Whenever a child came into her power she would kill it, cook it and eat it, and that made a real feast-day for her. (You ought to know too, that witches like this have red eyes and can't see very far, but they have a sense of smell as fine as animals, so they know when human-beings are getting close. Indeed, when Hansel and Gretel were near she had laughed wickedly and said to herself mockingly, "Two more for me. They'll not get away!")

Early the next morning, before the children were awake, the old woman got up and when she saw them sleeping there so pretty, with their round red cheeks, she muttered to herself, "That'll make a nice juicy morsel," and she grasped Hansel with her dry, bony hand and carried him off to a little stable and locked him in behind a barred door—he could cry as much as he liked, it would do no good. Then she went to Gretel, shook her awake and shouted out, "Get up, lazybones, get the water and boil up something nice for your brother, sitting out there in the pen where he's going to get fat—because when he's fat I'm going to eat him." Straight away Gretel started to cry, but it was all in vain; she had to do what the evil witch demanded.

Now came a time when the best of everything was cooked for Hansel—but Gretel got nothing but crab-shells. Every morning the old woman would sneak down to the little pen and call, "Hansel, poke out your finger so that I can feel if you're fat enough yet." But Hansel would poke out a little bone, and the old woman, whose eyes were dimming, couldn't see what it was and thought it was Hansel's finger and was astonished that he never seemed to get any fatter. So after four weeks, with Hansel seemingly as thin as ever, impatience overcame her and she could wait no longer.

"Hey, there, Gretel," she called out to the girl. "Quick! Carry up some water—I shall butcher that Hansel tomorrow and boil him up whether he's plump or skinny or whatever!" Dearie, oh dear, how his little sister wailed when she had to fetch the water, and what great tears rolled down her cheeks!

"God! God! help us now if ever!" she cried. "If the wild beasts in the forest had eaten us, at least we'd have died together!"

"Stop your blubbering," said the old woman, "'twon't do you any good."

So early next morning Gretel had to go out and hang up the cauldron and light the fire. "But first of all we'll do some baking," said the old woman. "I've already heated the oven and kneaded the dough," and she shoved poor Gretel outside to the baking-oven, which now had great flames pouring out of it. "You creep in there," said the witch, "and see that it's warming up properly, so that we can slide in the bread (and when Gretel was inside she was going to shut the oven-door and bake her up, so that she could eat her too).

But Gretel realised what she had in mind and said, "I don't know how to do it. How can I get in there?"

"You little goose!" said the old woman, "the opening's big enough— look here, I could get in myself," and she scrabbled around and stuck her head into the baking-oven. Then Gretel gave her a great shove, so that she tumbled right in, slammed the iron door shut and dropped the bar. Whoo! what a howling—ugh! horrible!—but Gretel ran off and the wicked witch was left to be baked alive.

Straight as an arrow, Gretel ran to Hansel and opened his little pen, crying out, "Hansel, we're free—the old witch is dead!"—and Hansel sprang out, like a bird from a cage, when the door's opened. What a time they had—hugging each other, jumping around, kissing! And because there was nothing for them to be afraid of now, they went into the witch's house and found caskets full of pearls and jewels standing in every corner.

"These are better than little white pebbles!" said Hansel, and stuffed his pockets as full as he could: and Gretel said, "Well I'll take something home too," and she filled up her apron.

"But now we must be off," said Hansel, "to be sure we get out of this enchanted forest."

But after they'd walked for a couple of hours they came to a huge lake. "We can't get over that," said Hansel, "there's no bridge and no causeway."

"There's no ferry either," said Gretel. "But look! Over there's a little white duck, perhaps she'll help us over if I ask." And she called out,

> "Little duck, little duck, duckling dear,
>   Hansel and Gretel are standing here.
>   A path they lack, and a bridge they lack,
>   Please carry them over on your back."

And the duck swam up and Hansel climbed aboard and called his little sister to join him. "Oh no," answered Gretel, "the two of us'll be too heavy for the duck. She'll have to take us one at a time."

And that's what the kind little animal did and after they'd both landed safely on the other side and walked on for a little while they found themselves getting to know the forest better and better till at last they saw, far off, their father's house. Then they began to run, burst into the room and rushed to hug their father. (This poor man had never had a moment's peace since he'd left his children in the forest—and, as for his wife, she was dead.) Gretel emptied her apron so that the pearls and precious stones fell out and rolled around the room, and Hansel threw one handful after another out of his pockets to join them. So all their cares were at an end and they lived together in perfect happiness.

The tale is done
A mouse doth run.

(And whoever can catch it can make himself a huge great fur cap from it—so there!)

The Blue Light

Once upon a time there was a soldier who'd served his king faithfully for many long years. But when the wars were over and the soldier good for no further service (on account of the many wounds he'd had) the king said to him, "Right, you can go home now—I've got no more use for you. You'll get no more pay from me—pay's only for the ones that can give me something in return."

The soldier had no idea how he was going to earn his living. He left with a heavy heart and tramped the whole day long till, at evening, he came to a forest. As darkness fell he saw a light, which he went towards, and so came to a house where lived a witch.

"Give me a place to rest for the night and something to eat and drink," says he to her, "else I'm done for."

"Hoho!" says she, "and who gives anything to stray soldiers? Still—I'll take pity on you and take you in, so long as you do what I ask."

"Depends what it is," says the soldier.

"Dig my garden over in the morning."

Well, the soldier agreed to that and the next day he worked with all his strength, but couldn't get done by evening. "I can see very well," said the witch, "that you can't do any more today, so I'll put you up for another night and then tomorrow you can split and trim me a wagon-load of firewood." The soldier needed the whole day to do that and in the evening the witch proposed that he stay another night. "There's just one little job you can do for me tomorrow. Back of my house there's an old empty well and my lamp's fallen into it. It burns blue and never goes out—you can go down and fetch it for me."

So the next day the old woman took him to the well and let him down in a basket. He found the blue light and gave the signal for her to pull him up again. So she hauled him up to the top, but when he got close to the rim of the well she reached down to take the blue light.

"Oh, no," said he, realising her evil intentions, "you don't get the light till I'm standing with both feet on solid ground." But at that the witch flew into a rage, let him fall back into the well and cleared off.

The poor soldier fell down to the damp bottom of the well without hurting himself and the blue light went on burning—but how could that help him? It seemed clear enough to him that he was all set to die. For a while he sat there, then, without thinking, he felt in his pocket and found his old tobacco pipe that was still half-full. "Well that shall be my last comfort," he said to himself and pulled it out, lit it at the blue light and began to puff.

As the smoke drifted round in the hole there suddenly stood before him a little black mannikin who said, "Master, what is thy command?"

"What's my command?" asked the soldier, all amazed.

"I must do whatever thou desirest," said the little man.

"Oh," said the soldier, "good. Then first of all get me out of this well." The little man took him by the hand and led him through an underground passage (the soldier not forgetting to take the blue light, of course). On the way he showed him all the treasures that the witch had got together and stored away there, and the soldier took as much gold as he could carry.

When he got to the top, the soldier said to the mannikin, "Now, go on with you. Bind the old witch and take her before the magistrates," and not long after that she came tearing past, riding a wild cat and shrieking fit to freeze your blood. It didn't last long, though, and soon the little man was back.

"Judged and sentenced," said he, "and the witch already hangs from the gallows. Now, master, what is thy further command?"

"For the moment," answered the soldier, "you can go home, but be sure to be on hand when I call you."

"Thou needst do nothing," said the little mannikin, "but set thy pipe to the blue light, then shall I stand before thee." And straight away he disappeared from view.

The soldier now returned to the city he'd come from. He went to the best inn and had a fine suit of clothes made for himself. Then he ordered the innkeeper to fit out a room for him as splendid as possible. When all that was done and the soldier had moved in, he called up the black mannikin and said, "I served the king here faithfully but he turned me out and let me starve. Now I shall be revenged."

"What must I do?" asked the little one.

"Late this evening, when the king's daughter is in bed, bring her here asleep. She shall do my chores for me."

The little man said, "For me that is an easy thing, but for thee a dangerous one. Should all become known, it will go ill with thee."

When midnight had struck, the door of the soldier's room sprang open and the mannikin brought in the princess.

"Sa ho!" cried the soldier, "it's you is it! Well get to work! go on— fetch the broom, sweep up the place, sweep it up!"

When she'd done that he called her over to his chair, stretched out his feet towards her and said, "Come on, take off my boots." Then he threw them at her head and made her pick them up, clean them and polish them till they shone. But she did all these things that he ordered without grumbling, dumbly, and with half-closed eyes. Then, at first cock-crow, the little man carried her back to the royal palace and into her own bed.

The next morning, when the princess was up, she went to her father and told him she'd had a strange dream: "I was carried through the streets like lightning and brought to a soldier's room where I had to fetch and carry like a serving-maid—do all kinds of common jobs—sweep the room, clean the boots. It was only a dream, and yet I feel tired enough to have done it all."

"It's a dream that could be true," said the king. "Let me give you some advice. Fill your pocket with peas and make a little hole in it. If you're carried off again they'll drop out and leave a trail through the streets."

While the king said that though, the little man was standing invisible beside him, listening to everything. So that night, when again he carried the sleeping princess through the streets, there was indeed a scatter of peas falling from her pocket, but they left no trail, because the cunning little man had spread peas in all the other streets beforehand. And once again the princess had to act the serving-maid till cock-crow.

The next morning the king sent out his men to follow the trail—but all in vain, for in every street raggedy children were gathering up the peas and saying, "Look! it's rained peas in the night."

"Well we'll have to think of something else," said the king. "Keep your slippers on when you go to bed, and before you come home hide one of them. I'll find that soon enough." But the little black mannikin heard this plan too and when the soldier ordered him that evening to bring back the princess again he tried to stop him, said that he knew no counter to this trick and if the slipper was found it would go ill with him.

"You do what you're told," answered the soldier, and the princess had to work like a serving-maid for a third night. But before she was carried home she hid one of her slippers under the bed.

The next morning the king mounted a search through the whole town for his daughter's slipper. It was found at the soldier's lodging and the soldier himself (who had fled the town on the advice of the little man) was caught and thrown into prison. In the course of his flight he'd forgotten his best help—the blue light and the gold—and he'd only got a single ducat in his pocket. But as he stood at the window of his cell, all loaded down with chains, he saw one of his old comrades go past. He banged at the shutter and as the fellow came up he asked him to be so good as to fetch the little bundle he'd left at his lodgings. "I'll give you a ducat for it," he said.

The servant of the blue light goes about his task

The old comrade ran off and brought him what he wanted. Then, as soon as the soldier was alone again, he lit up his pipe and caused the little mannikin to appear. "Have no fear," said he to his master, "go thou where they lead thee, and let all happen as it will. Only take the blue light with thee." So on the next day judgement was pronounced on the soldier, and, although he'd committed no crime, he was condemned to death.

When he was led out he asked the king for a last boon.

"What sort of a boon?" asked the king.

"Only to be able to smoke a pipe on the way."

"You may smoke half a dozen pipes," said the king, "but don't think I'm going to grant you your life."

So the soldier drew out his pipe and set it to the blue light, and no sooner had a couple of smoke-rings gone up into the air than the little mannikin appeared with a small cudgel in his hand.

"Master, what is thy command?"

"Knock down the false judge there and his constables for me—and don't spare the king either who's treated me so badly."

So the little mannikin leapt about like lightning, zick zack, here and there, and whoever he touched with his cudgel fell to the ground and didn't dare get up again. As for the king, though, he was terrified. He lay down and begged for mercy and—in exchange for his life—he gave the soldier his kingdom and the hand of his daughter in marriage.

Six Men Go Far Together in the Wide World

Once upon a time there was a man who was skilled in many devices. He served in the wars and showed much daring and courage, but when the wars were over they gave him a fond farewell and four penn'orth of wages to see him on his way.

"Wait a minute," says he, "that's not good enough for me; once I get hold of the right people I shall see to it that the king hands over the treasures of his whole nation." And full of anger he went off into the forest, where he saw a fellow standing who'd just pulled up six trees as if they were blades of corn.

"How would you like to serve me," he says to him, "and travel along with me?"

"Fine," says the other, "but first of all I must take home this little faggot of wood for my mother," and he took one of the trees, wound it round the five others, put the faggot on his shoulder and carried it off. Then he came back again and went off along with his master who said,

"The two of us should go far in the wide world."

After they'd gone along for a while they came to a huntsman kneeling down with his rifle levelled to take aim. The master says to him, "Huntsman what are you shooting at?" and the huntsman says:

"Two miles away there's a fly sitting on the branch of an oak-tree, I'm going to shoot him in the left eye."

"Oho! you must come with me!" says the man. "We three should go far together in the wide world." The huntsman was ready enough and went along with them till they came to seven windmills whose sails were hurtling round even though there was no wind from east or west and not a leaf stirring on the trees.

Then the man says, "What on earth's driving these windmills, there's no sign of a breeze," and he went on a bit with his servants and after they'd walked a couple of miles they saw a fellow sitting in a tree holding one nostril and blowing through the other.

"Lordy me! what are you doing up there?" says the man, and the other fellow answers:

"Do you see—two miles over there there are seven windmills, I'm blowing to make them go round."

"Oho! you must come with me," says the man. "We four should go far together in the wide world."

So the blower got down and went along with them, and after a time they saw a chap standing there on one leg with the other unbuckled and lying on the ground beside him. So the master says, "You look to have made yourself very comfortable."

"Ah, I'm the runner," says the other, "and I've unbuckled that leg so that I shan't leap off too quickly. When I run with two legs it's faster than a bird flying."

"Oho! you must come with me. We five should go far together in the wide world."

So he went along with them and it wasn't long before they met a fellow wearing a hat, but tilted right over one ear. So the master says to him, "Manners! manners! don't hang your hat on one ear like that, you look like a right tomfool."

"Ooh I daren't do that," says the other, "for if I put my hat straight there'll be a great frost and the birds'll freeze in the sky and fall down dead to the ground."

"Oho! you must come with me," says the master. "We six should go far together in the wide world."

So the six of them went to a city where the king had made it known that whoever raced with his daughter and beat her should marry her; but if he lost then he'd lose his head. So the man presented himself and said, "But I want one of my servants to do the running for me," to which the king answered, "Then you've pledged his life too. Your head and his head against victory."

Well, when it was all fixed and settled, the man buckled on the runner's other leg and said to him, "Now get a move on and see that we win."

It had to be agreed that whoever was the first to bring some water from a distant well should be the winner. So the runner got a jug and the king's daughter got another jug, and they both set off running at the same time. But within a moment, with the princess only a few steps on her way, there wasn't an onlooker who could see anything of the runner—it was like nothing so much as the wind tearing by. In no time at all he'd got to the well, filled up the jug with water and turned back home. But half way back he was overcome with weariness, so he set down the jug, lay down on the ground and went to sleep. But he'd been careful to use a horse's skull that was lying there for a pillow so that he'd have a hard head-rest and would wake up pretty soon.

Meanwhile the princess, who was a good runner (good, that is, for an ordinary mortal), had reached the well and was hurrying back with her jugful of water. But when she saw the runner lying there sleeping she was overjoyed and said, "The enemy is delivered into my hands," and she tipped up his jug and ran on.

Well all would have been lost there and then had not the huntsman with the sharp eyes fortunately been standing up atop the castle watching all that had been going on. "That princess shan't get us that way," he said, loaded his rifle and fired with such skill that he shot the horse's skull from under the runner's head without doing him the least harm. The runner woke up at once, jumped in the air and saw that his jug was empty and the princess already far ahead. But he didn't despair. He ran back to the well with his jug, filled up with a fresh lot of water and was back home a good ten minutes before the princess. "See here," said he, "that made me lift my legs; it wasn't worth calling a race to start with."

Naturally it upset the king (and it upset his daughter a good deal more) that she should be carried off by a common soldier, and a discharged one at that; so they put their heads together to decide how they could be rid of him and all his companions.

"Don't worry," said the king, "I've found the means. They won't be coming back home again." And to them he said, "Well, gentlemen, you must all get together for a celebration. Eat! Drink!" and he led them to a room with a floor made of iron, and with iron doors and iron bars fixed over the windows.

A table had been put in this room, laid with rich foods, and the king said to them, "Go on in; enjoy yourselves." But once they were inside he had the doors locked and bolted. Then he sent for the cook and ordered him to get a furnace going under the room till the iron grew red-hot.

Well the cook did all that so that the six fellows in the room, sitting round the table, began to feel pretty warm and they thought it must be from eating. But as the heat got worse and worse and they tried to get out and found the doors and windows bolted they realised that the king's intentions had not been of the best and that he was out to suffocate them.

"He won't succeed though," said the chap with the hat, "I'll raise such a frost that the fire'll feel ashamed of itself and creep away." And he put his hat straight on his head and straight away there fell a frost that drove off all the heat and made the plates and the food begin to freeze.

So now—after a few hours had passed and the king thought them all shrivelled up he had the door opened and went to look at them himself. But when the door swung wide there stood all six, sound in wind and limb, saying how glad they were to be able to get out and warm themselves because the food was all frozen to the plates on account of the fearful cold.

Full of rage, the king went down to the cook and berated him and demanded to know why he hadn't carried out his orders. The cook, though, answered, "It's hot enough there, see for yourself." And the king saw a huge, great fire was roaring beneath the iron room and he realised that he couldn't come at the six in that way.

Now the king began to think of new ways to be rid of his hated guests. He summoned their master and said, "If you'll take gold instead of my daughter you shall have as much as you want."

"Indeed yes, Lord King," he answered, "if you'll give me as much as my servants can carry I'll not be after your daughter any more."

The king was satisfied with that, and the man went on, "So I'll come back in a fortnight and fetch the gold." Then he called up all the tailors throughout the kingdom and had them sitting down for fourteen days sewing a sack. And when it was done the strong man who could tear up trees had to take the sack over his shoulder and go to the king.

Then the king said, "Who's that hefty fellow with a bale of canvas on his shoulder as big as a house?" He was properly shocked and said to himself, "How much gold is he going to drag away?" Then he called for a ton of gold, which was brought in by sixteen of his strongest men, but the strong man grasped it with one hand, poked it in the sack and said, "Why don't you bring as much again? That lot hardly covers the bottom."

And so gradually the king had all his treasure brought out, and the strong man stowed it all in the sack and the sack still wasn't half full. "More!" he cried. "More! these few bits won't fill anything." So seven thousand wagons full of gold had to be driven in from all parts of the kingdom, and the strong man stowed these into his sack with the oxen and their harnesses and all.

"I won't keep much of an eye on it," he said. "I'll take what comes, just to get the sack full." And when everything was packed in, there was still room for more, but he said, "Enough's enough; people tie sacks up when they're not properly full," and he humped it on to his back and set off with his comrades.

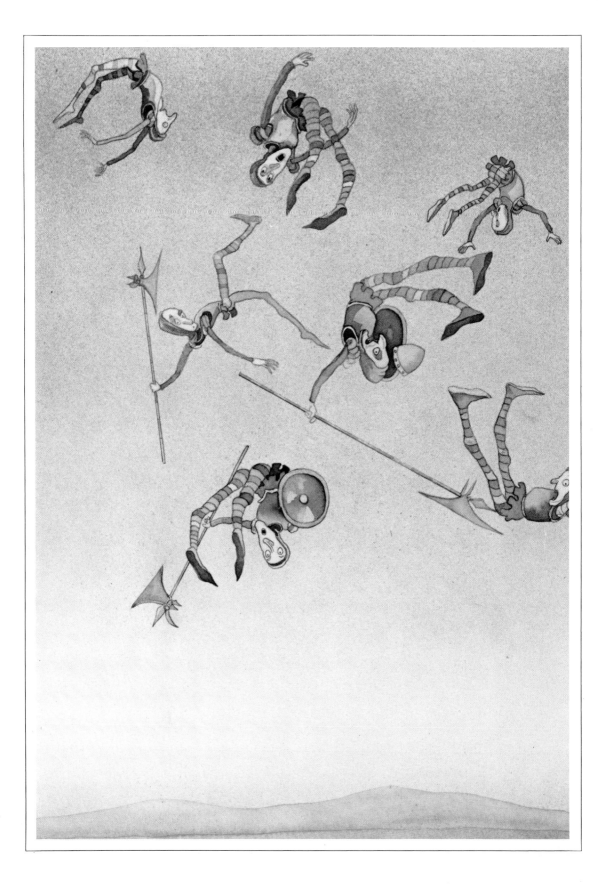

Now when the king saw how this one single man was carting off the whole kingdom's wealth he was furious and ordered out his cavalry. They had orders to hunt down the six and seize the sack from the strong man. So it was that two regiments soon overtook them and called out to them, "You are prisoners! Lay down the sack of gold or you'll all be hacked to pieces!"

"What's that you say?" said nose-blower. "We're prisoners? Better to say you're all going dancing on air!" And he closed one nostril and blew at the two regiments through the other, and they all fluttered away into the blue sky, some that way, some this. One sergeant-major cried for mercy— he'd had nine wounds and was a brave fellow who didn't deserve such disgrace. So the nose-blower eased off a bit so that he came down to earth again without harm, and he said to him, "Very well, go home to your king and tell him that if he'd like to send some more cavalry I'd like to blow them all up into the air."

When the king heard this news he said, "Let the fellows go, there's something about that lot." So the six companions brought home their riches, divided them up and lived contentedly to the end of their days.

How the sixth man finds his way in the world

Rumpelstiltskin

Once upon a time there was a miller—poor enough, but he had a beautiful daughter. Now it so happened that he got to speak with the king and, to give himself a bit of an air, he said, "I've got a daughter can spin straw into gold."

Then the king said to the miller, "You know, that's a craft that takes my fancy. If your daughter's as clever as you say she is, bring her along to my palace in the morning and we'll put her to the test."

When the girl was brought to him he led her into a chamber that was full of straw, gave her a wheel and spindle and said, "Now, get to work, and if this straw hasn't been spun into gold between tonight and tomorrow morning early, you must die." Then he locked up the room with his own hand and she was left there alone.

Well, there sat the poor miller's daughter and didn't know what to do to save herself. She hadn't the first idea how anyone could spin straw into gold and her misery grew and grew till she finally burst out crying.

Suddenly the door opened and a tiny little man came in and said, "Good evening, Miss Miller's Daughter, why all these tears?"

146

"Aaah," said the girl, "I've got to spin straw into gold and I don't know how to do it."

And the little man said, "Well, what'll you give me if I spin it for you?"

"My necklace," said the girl. So the little man took the necklace, sat himself down at the wheel, and whirr, whirr, whirr, three times round and the bobbin was full. Then he put another one on and whirr, whirr, whirr, three times round, and that was full too—and so it went on till morning, and there was all the straw spun, and there were all the bobbins full of gold.

At sun-up along came the king and whem he saw the gold he was amazed and overjoyed—but his heart grew greedy for more. He had the miller's daughter brought to another chamber full of straw—bigger than the last—and ordered her to spin all that in a single night if she loved her life.

The girl didn't know what to do and wept, but then the door opened once more and the little man appeared and said, "What'll you give me if I spin this straw into gold?"

"The ring from my finger," answered the girl—so the little man took the ring and started whirring away again with the wheel and, by morning, he'd spun all the straw into glittering gold.

The king was pleased beyond all measure at the sight of this, and yet was still not gorged with gold. He had the miller's daughter brought to an even bigger chamber full of straw and said, "All this is for spinning tonight, and if you succeed you shall be my wife." ("Even if she is a miller's daughter," he thought to himself, "I'll never find a richer woman in the whole wide world.")

When the girl was alone the little man came for a third time and said, "What'll you give me if I spin this straw yet again?"

"I've nothing more to give," answered the girl.

"Then promise me your first child if you get to be queen."

"Who knows if that'll ever happen," thought the miller's daughter, and, since she didn't see how she could help herself anyway, she promised what the little man wanted, and the little man once more spun the straw into gold, and when the king came in the morning and found

everything as he desired, he married her and the beautiful miller's daughter became a queen.

More than a year later she brought a beautiful child into the world, but with never a thought about the little man. Then suddenly he came into her room and said, "Now, give me what you promised."

The queen was terrified, and offered the little man all the riches of the kingdom if he would let her child be, but the little man said, "No. A living thing is dearer to me than all the treasures of the world." So the queen began to take on, weeping and wailing, till the little man took pity on her.

"I'll give you three days' grace," he said, "and if you can find my name in that time then you shall keep your child."

All night the queen pondered over all the names she'd ever heard, and she sent out a messenger through all the countryside to make inquiries here, there and everywhere about what kind of names there were. When the little man came next day she began with Caspar, Melchior, Balthazar, and said all the names she knew in a great long string, but to each of them the little man said, "That's not me."

The second day she asked everyone around the place what their names were, and offered the little man the weirdest and most unusual names. "Are you by any chance called Gobbles? Or Ribbingtop? Or Schickelgruber?"; but he always answered "That's not me."

On the third day the messenger returned with the report: "Not a single new name could I find. But when I came to the corner of a wood on a high mountain, where the fox and the hare say goodnight to each other, I saw a little house, and in front of the house was a fire, and round the fire there was a ridiculous little man, jumping and hopping about on one leg and yelling:

'Today I bake, tomorrow brew,
  The next day, princeling, come for you.
  What a very good thing that none shall claim
  That Rumpelstiltskin is my name.'"

Well, you may imagine how glad the queen was when she head *that*, and when the little man came in soon after and said, "Now, Lady

Rumpelstiltskin at the spinning wheel

Queen, what's my name?" she asked first, "Are you Jim?"

"No."

"Are you Fred?"

"No."

"Then how about Rumpelstiltskin!"

"The devil told you that! The devil told you that," shrieked the little man, and in his fury he stamped his right foot deep into the ground, right up to his waist, then, foaming at the mouth, he grabbed his left foot in both hands and tore himself apart right down the middle.

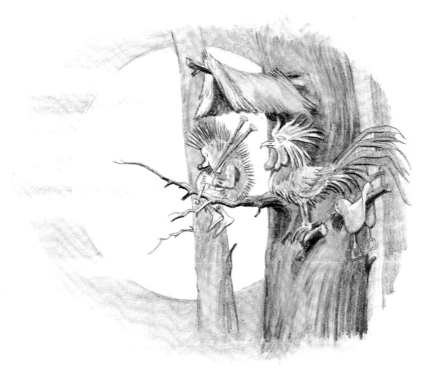

Hans My Hedgehog

Once upon a time there was a farmer. He'd got plenty of goods and gear, but however rich they made him seem he still lacked one thing to be completely happy: he and his wife had no children. Often enough when he went down to the town with the other farmers they'd make fun of him and want to know why he hadn't got any children, and in the end he got mad, and when he came home he said, "I'll get a child even if it's only a hedgehog."

Well, a child his wife did have, and its top half was hedgehog and its bottom half boy, and when his wife saw it she was appalled and said, "There! Look at that! You've got us cursed."

Then the man said, "Well, it can't be helped. The little fellow will have to be christened, but we can hardly ask anyone to stand godfather."

And his wife: "What's more, we can't christen him anything but Hans My Hedgehog."

When the christening was over the priest said, "I can see you're not

151

going to fit *him* into an ordinary bed, on account of his prickles"—so a bit of straw was sorted out behind the stove and Hans My Hedgehog was laid on that. Nor could he take his mother's milk either, because he would have jabbed her with his prickles. So he lay there, behind the stove, eight years, and his father was fed up with him and thought, "If only he'd die." But he didn't die—just stayed there, lying.

Now it so happened that a fair came to the town and the farmer was going to go. He asked his wife what he should bring back. "A cut of meat and a few small loaves for the housekeeping," she said.

Then he asked the maid, and she wanted some slippers and clock-stockings.

And lastly he said, "Well, Hans My Hedgehog, what can I do for you?"

"Daddy," says he, "bring me back a bagpipes."

So when the farmer came back home again he gave his wife what he'd bought for her—meat and rolls—he gave the maid her slippers and clock-stockings, and, last of all, he went behind the stove and gave Hans My Hedgehog the bagpipes.

And when Hans My Hedgehog got these bagpipes he said, "Daddy, just go down to the blacksmith's and have my old cock-rooster shod, then I'll ride away and never come back again." His father was delighted that at last he was to be rid of him and he had the old cock shod, and when he was done Hans My Hedgehog got up on his back and rode away, taking with him some pigs and asses that he wanted to look after in the forest.

When he got to the forest he made the cock fly him up into a tall tree, and there he sat and looked after his asses and pigs. Many a long year he sat there until his flocks had grown and grown—but his father knew nothing about him at all. And while he sat up in his tree he would blow his bagpipes and make wonderful music.

Now one day a king came riding by who'd got himself lost, and he heard this music. He was amazed at it and sent his servant off with orders to look around to see where the music came from. So he looked around, but saw nothing but a little creature sitting up in a tree which seemed to be a cock-rooster with a hedgehog sitting on it, and that was what was making the music. So the king said to his servant that he should ask why he was sitting there and if he knew the way back to his kingdom.

So Hans My Hedgehog climbed down from his tree and said he'd show him the way so long as the king would promise to assign to him whatever it was that first came to meet him from the royal court when he got back home. "I can do that easily enough," thought the king. "Hans My Hedgehog has got no brains and I can write down what I like." So the king took pen and ink and wrote down something or other, and when he'd done, Hans My Hedgehog showed him the way and he made his way merrily home.

Now the king had a daughter, and when she saw him coming in the distance she was so overjoyed that she ran out to him and kissed him. Then he thought of Hans My Hedgehog and told her how things had gone with him and how he'd had to sign over to a strange beast whatever first came to meet him when he got home—and this beast had been sitting astride a cock as though it were a horse, making wonderful music. For his part, of course, he'd just written that the creature wasn't to have these things, because poor old Hans My Hedgehog couldn't read anyhow. The princess was very glad to hear that and said it was just as well, since she'd never have gone.

Hans My Hedgehog continued to look after his asses and pigs, showed never a care in the world, sat up in his tree and blew down his bagpipes. But it so happened that another king came riding with his grooms and servants, and *he'd* got himself lost too, and didn't know how to get home because the forest was so deep. He likewise heard the beautiful music from way off and asked his groom to go and find out what it might be. So the groom came along under the tree and saw the cock-rooster sitting there with Hans My Hedgehog in the saddle. The groom asked him what on earth he was doing up there.

"Me? I'm looking after my asses and my pigs. But what about you? What do you want?" The groom explained that they'd got themselves lost and couldn't find their way back to their kingdom unless he could show it them. So Hans My Hedgehog and the cock got down from the tree and said to the old king he'd show him the way so long as he'd give him for his own whatever first came to meet him outside his royal castle when he got back home. The king said "Yes" and set his hand to the agreement that Hans My Hedgehog should have it. When that was done Hans My Hedgehog rode ahead on his cock-rooster and showed him the way, and the king rode merrily back to his kingdom.

There was much joy at court when the king came home, and his one and only daughter—who was very beautiful—ran to meet him, put her arms round his neck and kissed him, so glad to have her old father back again. She too, just like the other, asked him where in the world he'd been so long, and he told her he'd got himself lost and might never have got back at all, except that, as he was riding through a deep wood, somebody—half hedgehog, half man, sitting astride a cock in a tall tree and making wonderful music—had helped him forward and shown him the way. For his part, though, he'd promised to give him whatever first came to meet him from his court, and that was she, and he was very sorry for it. But his daughter promised she would gladly go with him when he came, for love of her old father.

Hans My Hedgehog went on looking after his pigs, and his pigs bred more pigs, till they got to be so many that the forest was full of them. Hans My Hedgehog then decided not to live in the forest any more and he sent a message to his father saying they should clear out all the stables in the village because he was coming with such a huge herd that anyone could slaughter as wanted to slaughter. His father was very woebegone when he heard this, because he thought Hans My Hedgehog was dead long ago.

But Hans My Hedgehog climbed on his cock-rooster, drove the pigs before him into the village and let battle commence. Whoosh! There was a butchering and slaughtering that you could hear ten miles off—and when it was over Hans My Hedgehog said, "Daddy, have my cock-rooster shod once more at the blacksmith's and then I'll be off and never come back in all my born days." So Daddy had the cock-rooster shod and was delighted that Hans My Hedgehog wouldn't be coming back again.

Hans My Hedgehog rode off to the first kingdom. Here the king had given orders that if anyone turned up riding on a cock and toting bagpipes then everybody must turn to and shoot him, slash him and stab him so that he shouldn't enter the castle. So when Hans My Hedgehog came riding along there, they all rushed out at him with their bayonets, but he set spurs to his cock, flew up over the gate and in at the king's window, where he got down and called out that he must give him what he'd promised, otherwise he'd kill both king and daughter.

At this the king spoke all soft and soapy to his daughter: perhaps she'd like to go out there and meet him and save both of their lives. So she got dressed all in white and her father gave her a coach with six horses and with splendid servants, and lots of goods and chattels. She got in and sat down with Hans My Hedgehog, with his cock and bagpipes next to her. They said their farewells and drove off, and the king thought never to see her again. It wasn't the best of thoughts though, for they hadn't gone more than a bit of the way from the town when Hans My Hedgehog tore off all her fine clothes and rolled on her with his prickles, saying, "That's the reward for your falseness. Get on with you, I'll not have more of you," and he chased her back home, where she was mocked for the rest of her days.

But Hans My Hedgehog rode away on his cock-rooster, with his bagpipes, to the second kingdom whose king he'd helped in finding the way. This one, though, had ordered that if anyone came like Hans My Hedgehog they should present arms, lead him freely along, shout Huzza, and bring him into the royal castle. When the princess saw him, however, she was aghast, because he looked so strange, but she thought there was nothing to be done, she'd promised her father. So Hans My Hedgehog was given a royal welcome by her, was married to her and had to go and sit at the royal table with her, and she sat at his side and they ate and drank.

When evening came and time for them to go to bed she grew terrified at the thought of his prickles; but he said no need to be afraid, no harm would come to her; and he said to the old king he should place four men on guard outside the chamber-door and they should build a great fire,

and when he went into the chamber and sought to lie down he would creep out of his hedgehog skin and leave it lying by the bed; then the men should charge into the room and hurl it into the fire and stay by it till it was all consumed.

Now, when the clock struck eleven he went into the chamber, stripped off the hedgehog-skin and let it lie by the bed. Then the men came in, took it up and quickly threw it into the fire; and when the fire had consumed it he was freed and lay there in the bed formed whole as a man—but coal-black as though he'd been burnt. The king sent for his physician, who washed him with gentle salves and with balsam and he turned white, and a fine young man. When the princess saw him she was overcome with happiness, and the next morning they got up full of joy, ate and drank, and their marriage was properly celebrated and Hans My Hedgehog received the kingdom for his own at the hands of the old king.

After some years had passed he rode with his wife to see his father and told him he was his son. But his father said he had no son—true, he *had* had one, but that one had been like a hedgehog, stuck all over with prickles, and he'd gone off into the world. So the young man explained all that had happened and his old father rejoiced and went with him into his kingdom.

Snip, snap, snover
That story's over.

Hans my Hedgehog claims his due

The Goose-girl

Once upon a time there lived an old queen whose husband had been dead many a long year. And she had a beautiful daughter. In course of growing up this girl was promised to a king's son far away in another country. Now when the time came for her to be married and the child had to set off for that far land, the old woman packed her up great quantities of precious gems and jewels, gold and silver, goblets and trinkets—in short, everything that ought to be in a royal bride's dowry—for she loved her child from the bottom of her heart. She also gave her a young chamber-maid, to ride with her and to hand the bride to the bridegroom, and each of them had a horse for the journey, but the princess' horse was called Falada and he could talk.

When the time came for them to leave, the old mother took herself off to her bed-chamber, brought out a little knife and cut her finger with it so that she bled. Then she held a little white rag under the cut and let three drops of blood fall on to it. This she gave to her daughter, and said, "Child, my dear child, look after this with all your care, you will need it on your journey."

Then the two of them made a sorrowful farewell. The princess pushed the little rag between her breasts, mounted her horse and rode off to her bridegroom. But after they'd ridden for an hour she was overcome by a raging thirst and she said to her chamber-maid, "Get down and take my cup that you've got with you and fill it with water from the brook; I'd like to have a drink."

"If you're thirsty," said the chamber-maid, "get down yourself—lie down and drink at the stream—I'll not be servant of yours."

So the princess dismounted, driven by her furious thirst, bent over the water in the brook and drank—no question of her drinking from her golden cup.

"God! God!" she said, and the three drops of blood answered:

"If thy mother only knew,
Her heart would surely break in two."

But the princess was a humble creature. She said nothing and climbed back on her horse.

On they rode, some miles further. But the day was warm; the sun burned down; and soon she was thirsty again. Since, at that moment, they'd come to a river she called once more to her chamber-maid, "Get down, and fetch me a drink in my golden cup." (For she'd already forgotten the other's evil words.)

But the chamber-maid said more proudly than ever, "If you want a drink see about it on your own, I'll not be servant of yours."

So the princess got down, driven by her violent thirst, bent over the rippling water, wept, and said, "God! God!"—and the drops of blood again answered:

"If thy mother only knew,
Her heart would surely break in two."

And as she drank there, leaning over the water, the little rag with the blood fell from between her breasts and floated away on the water without her ever noticing it, so great was her sorrow. But the chamber-maid had seen, and rejoiced at the power that she would now have over the young bride—for, since she'd lost the drops of blood, she'd become weak and defenceless.

So when she came back and sought to mount Falada, her horse, the chamber-maid said, "I'm the one belongs on Falada; you belong on this old hack," and she had to be content with that. Then the chamber-maid gave harsh orders for her to get out of her royal apparel and put on the servant's greasy clothes, and, to cap all, she had to swear under the wide heavens that she would say nothing of all this to anyone at the royal court; and if she hadn't taken this oath she would have been murdered on the spot. But Falada saw everything, and laid it up in his mind.

So now the chamber-maid climbed up on Falada and the true bride on the nag and they went on their way till at last they came to the king's castle. There was great rejoicing at their arrival and the prince leapt to meet them, lifted the chamber-maid from her horse, believing her to be his bride. She was led up the staircase, and as for the true princess, she had to stop below. But the old king looked down on her through his window, saw her standing there in the courtyard, and saw how fine-featured she was—delicate and beautiful. So he went straight away to the royal apartments and asked the bride about this girl that she'd brought with her, standing down there in the courtyard. Who was she?

"It's someone I picked up for company on the way. Give the girl some work to do instead of letting her stand about idle down there."

But the old king had no work to give her and couldn't think of anything, till at last he said, "Well—I've got this little lad who looks after the geese, she can help him." (This lad was called Curdie—which is short for Conrad—and the true bride had indeed to help him with the geese.)

Soon after this the false bride said to the prince, "Dearest love, please do me a little kindness," and he answered, "Whatever you wish."

"Very well then—send for the knacker and have him chop the head off that horse I came on—it was a nuisance all the way here." (In truth, though, she was afraid the horse might tell how she'd changed herself with the princess.) Things had now gone so far that there was no getting away from it: faithful Falada must die.

But the true princess heard about it and she secretly promised the knacker a piece of gold—which she would pay him—if he did her a small service. For in the town there was a huge, gloomy gateway, which she had to go through every morning and evening with the geese. Here, under this dark gateway, he might nail up Falada's head, so that she could see him more than once again. The knacker's boy promised to do this, hacked off the horse's head and nailed it fast beneath the dark gateway.

Early in the morning, as she and Curdie went out through the gate, she said as they passed,

"O thou, Falada, hanging there,"

and the head answered,

"O thou, young princess, ganging there,
  If thy mother only knew,
  Her heart would surely break in two."

Then, silently, she went out beyond the town and they drove the geese across the common. And when she came to a meadow she sat down and loosened her hair, which was pure gold, and little Curdie saw it and loved how it glittered, and he wanted to pull out a couple of strands. So she said,

"Blow little breeze from a great way off,
  Blow little Curdie's top-knot off.
  Let him chase after it, over the plain,
  Till I'm combed and braided and settled again."

And there blew up such a strong wind that it took Curdie's cap off his head and blew it across half the countryside, and after it he had to go. And when he got back again she'd done with all her combing and coiling and not a hair could he come by. That made him cross and he wouldn't say a word to her, and in that way they looked after the geese together till evening when they went back home.

The next morning when they drove their geese through the dark gateway the girl said,

"O thou, Falada, hanging there,"

and the head answered,

161

> "O thou, young princess, ganging there,
>   If thy mother only knew,
>   Her heart would surely break in two."

And out on the common she sat down again in the pasture and began to comb out her hair, and Curdie ran up and tried to grab some, but she said quickly,

> "Blow little breeze from a great way off,
>   Blow little Curdie's top-knot off.
>   Let him chase after it, over the plain,
>   Till I'm combed and braided and settled again."

And the wind blew, and blew his cap off his head, far away, so that Curdie had to run after it, and when he came back again she was well finished with her hair and not a strand of it could he get; and in that way they looked after the geese till evening.

But when evening came, and after they'd got home, Curdie went before the old king and said, "I'm not looking after geese any more with *her*."

"Why ever not?" asked the old king.

"Hey, she's a bloody nuisance the whole day long!"

So the old king ordered him to say how things went with her, and Curdie said, "Well, in the morning, when we go under the dark gate with the flock, there's a great nag's head on the wall, and she says to it,

> "O thou, Falada, hanging there,"

and the head answers,

> "O thou, young princess, ganging there,
>   If thy mother only knew,
>   Her heart would surely break in two."

And Curdie went on to tell what happened in the goose-meadow and how he had to keep running around after his cap.

The old king commanded him to drive the geese out again next day, and when it was morning he sat himself down behind the dark gate and

heard how she talked with Falada's head. Then he went after her on to the common and hid himself in a bush in the pasture. There he saw soon enough with his own eyes how the goose-girl and the goose-boy drove along the flock and how, after a while, she sat down and loosened her hair that shone with splendour. At the same time she said once more,

> "Blow little breeze from a great way off,
>   Blow little Curdie's top-knot off.
>   Let him chase after it, over the plain,
>   Till I'm combed and braided and settled again."

And a puff of wind came and carried off Curdie's cap, so that he had to run miles to get it, and the girl went on combing and braiding her locks—and the old king watched it all. Then he returned home, all unnoticed, and when the goose-girl got back in the evening he called her to one side and asked her what she was up to?

"I may not tell you, and I may not tell any man my sorrow, for thus have I sworn under the wide heavens, else had I been killed."

He urged and urged her and gave her no peace but he could get nothing out of her. So he said, "Well, if you won't tell me, go and tell your sorrow to the iron stove," and he left.

So she crept into the great iron stove, began to weep and wail and poured out her heart, saying, "There am I now, forsaken by all the world—and yet I am the daughter of a king. And a false chamber-maid has forced me by her power to set aside my royal apparel and has taken my place beside my bridegroom, while I have to do the common tasks of a goose-girl.

> "If my mother only knew,
>   Her heart would surely break in two."

But the old king was standing outside by the stove-pipe, lurking, and listening to what she said, and now he came back in the room and called her to get out of the stove. Then she was given royal clothes to wear and she was so beautiful it seemed a miracle. The old king sent for his son and revealed to him that he'd got a wrongful bride—she was really a chamber-maid, and the true one was standing here, the goose-girl that was.

The young prince was glad with all his heart when he saw how beautiful and virtuous she was, and a great feast was ordered to which everyone was invited—good friends all. At the head of the table sat the bridegroom, with the princess on one side of him and the chamber-maid on the other, but the chamber-maid was dazzled by it all and no longer recognised the princess in her glittering regalia.

Now when they had eaten and drunk and were all feeling very comfortable the old king set the chamber-maid a riddle as to what such and such a person was worth who had betrayed her master in such and such a way—and he told her the whole course of events and asked, "What judgement does she deserve?"

And the false bride said, "She's worth nothing better than to be taken out stark naked and stuck in a barrel banged through with sharp nails, and two white horses to be harnessed to it so that they can drag her from one street to another till she's dead."

"That is you," said the old king. "You have pronounced your own sentence and according to that you will be dealt with."

And once the judgement was carried out the young prince married the right bride and both reigned over their kingdom in peace and happiness.

Boots of Buffalo Leather

A soldier who's not afraid of anything doesn't give a damn for anything either. Well—there was just such a one who'd been paid off, and since he'd learned nothing and hence was good for nothing he wandered around begging off respectable folk. An old army-cloak hung round his shoulders and he'd also managed to keep hold of a pair of riding-boots made of buffalo-hide.

One day he was going cross-country, without troubling himself too much about whither or where, till at last he found himself in a forest. He didn't know where he was, but there on the trunk of a chopped tree he saw a man sitting, well-dressed and wearing a green hunting-jacket. The soldier shook him by the hand, lowered himself down on to the grass beside him and stretched out his legs.

"That's a fine pair o' boots you got there, very 'andsomely polished," he said to the huntsman, "but if you 'ad to travel around like me they wouldn't last you long. Now look at mine—those there are made of buffalo leather, they've done me proud an' they'll keep on going through thick an' thin."

After a while the soldier stood up and said, "Well—can't 'ang

166

around—'unger drives us on. But see 'ere, Bruvver Smartyboots, whereabouts are you orf to?"

"To tell you the truth, I don't know myself," answered the huntsman. "I'm lost in this wood."

"Same for both of us then," said the soldier, "two peas in a pod. We'll keep together and look for a way out." The huntsman grinned a bit and they went on together till nightfall.

"Well, we're not getting out of this forest," said the soldier, "but still—there's a light shining in the distance over there; they ought to give us a bite."

They found it was a house built of stone. They knocked on the door which was opened by an old woman. "We're looking for a billet," said the soldier, "and something to line our bellies with—any road, mine's as empty as an old knapsack."

"Well, you can't stay here," said the old woman, "this is a robbers' house and you'd be wisest to get along before they all come home, because if they find you here you're done for."

"Can't be as bad as that," said the soldier. "I've been two days without so much as a crumb and I don't care now if I get done in here or starve to death in the forest. I'm coming in." The huntsman wasn't keen to follow him, but the soldier dragged him in by his sleeve: "Come on, me hearty, it won't come to hanging."

The old woman was sorry for them and said, "Creep in there behind the stove; if there's anything over I'll push it through to you when they're asleep."

Well, they'd hardly sat down in the their corner before twelve robbers came storming in, sat down at the table (which had already been laid) and hollered out for food. The old woman brought in a huge roast and the robbers got down to business. But when the smell of the food got into the soldier's nostrils he said to the huntsman, "I can't stand any more of this, I'm for the table."

"You'll get us murdered," said the huntsman, and grabbed his arm—but the soldier started coughing as loud as he could. When the robbers heard that they flung down their knives and forks, leapt up and found the two behind the stove.

"Oho, gents!" they shouted. "Sitting in the corner are you? Well what're you doing here? Spies are you? Well you just wait—we'll give you flying-lessons from the branch of a tree!"

"Now then, manners, manners," said the soldier. "I'm very hungry; give us a bite to eat, then you can do what you like."

The robbers were startled by this and their leader said, "I can see you're not afraid of much. You can have some supper if you want—but afterwards we'll have to kill you."

"That's as may be," said the soldier, and he sat down at the table and began to hack away merrily at the roast. "Come on, Bruvver Smartyboots, eat up!" he shouted to the huntsman. "You know you're just as hungry as me, and your missus has never roast you a better joint than this." But the huntsman wouldn't eat.

The robbers watched the soldier with amazement and said, "Well, 'e don't stand on ceremony, does 'e?"

When he'd finished he said, "Well that was very good, that was. Now what about a drink?"

The robber-chief was just in the mood for such a thing, so he called out to the old woman, "Get a bottle up from the cellar, and make it one of the best!" and it was the soldier who pulled out the cork with a loud pop, went over to the huntsman with the bottle and said, "Watch out now, Bruvver, and you'll see a bloody miracle. I'm going to drink the 'ealth of this lot good and proper." Then he brandished the bottle over the heads of the robbers, calling out, "You shall all live, but with your mouths open and your right hands up," and he took a good swig.

Hardly had he said that than they all sat motionless, like stone, with their mouths open and their right arms up in the air. Then the huntsman said to the soldier, "I can see you've got plenty more tricks, but come on now, let's go home."

"Oho, me hearty, we can't march away as quick as that—we've beaten the enemy, now for the booty. There they are sitting tight, with their mouths open from surprise, but they can't move till I say so. Come on, let's eat and drink." So the old woman had to fetch up another bottle of the best wine and the soldier didn't leave the table till he'd eaten enough for three days more.

At last, though, when dawn broke, he said, "Now's the time to strike camp, and to make sure we don't have a long march the old woman can show us the nearest way to town."

When they arrived there, the soldier went to his old mates and said, "Out there in the forest I've found a nest of gallows-birds—come on with me and we'll hoist it out," and the soldier led them off, and said to the huntsman, "You 've gotter come too so's you can see how they flap when we grab their toes."

He placed his troops all round the robbers, then he took the bottle, swallowed another great gulp, brandished it over them, and called out, "You shall all live!" And straight away they were able to move, but they were then thrown down and had their hands and feet tied up with rope. Then the soldier called for them to be thrown on to a cart, like sacks, and said, "Right—orf to the nick with 'em—and the huntsman took one of the men to one side and gave him an order too.

"Bruvver Smartyboots," said the soldier, "we've mounted a surprise attack on the enemy. We've done well for ourselves, now we'll march behind, easy, like the old camp-followers." But as they drew near the town the soldier saw how a crowd of people were pushing and shoving outside the gates, cheering wildly and waving green branches in the air. And he saw all the royal bodyguard come tramping out. "What's all this then?" says he to the huntsman in amazement.

"Why, don't you know," answers the other, "today's the day when the king returns home—he's been away from the country a long time and everyone's coming to greet him."

"Well where is 'e then," says the soldier, "I can't see 'im."

"He's here," answers the huntsman. "I'm the king, and I let them know I was coming."

Then he unfastened his hunting-jacket so that you could see his royal dress. The soldier was terrified, fell to his knees and begged forgiveness that, out of ignorance, he'd treated him as an equal—and called him such names into the bargain. But the king took him by the hand and said, "You're a brave soldier and you saved my life. I'll see to it that you never want for anything again—and if at any time you fancy a joint of roast as good as the one they served in the robbers' house, then you've only to come to the royal kitchen. But before you start drinking anyone's health you'd better get leave from me!"

The Three Golden Hairs of the Devil

Once upon a time there was a poor woman gave birth to a little boy, and because he had a caul on his head when he came into the world it was put about by way of a prophecy that he'd get the king's daughter for a wife when he was fourteen years old.

Now it so happened that soon after this the king came to the village, but no one knew he was king, and when he asked folk what was the news, they answered him, "There was a lad born lately with a caul on his head, and whatever such a one reckons to do he succeeds at. What's more, it's said that he'll get the king's daughter for a wife when he's fourteen years old."

Well the king—who was an evil-hearted fellow—was vexed at this prophecy and he went up to the parents, all friendly-like, and said, "Now you're poor folk, why don't you make your lad over to me. I'll look after him."

To start with, though, they wouldn't do it, but since the stranger offered them so much fine gold, and since they thought, "Anyway he's a luck-child, it'll all work out for the best," they finally agreed and handed the child over.

The king laid the baby in a box and rode off with him till he came to some deep water; then he tossed the box in and said to himself, "There, I've saved my daughter from an unlikely wooer." But the box didn't sink, but floated along like a little boat and never a drop of water came inside. It floated along like this till it came within a couple of miles of the king's great city, where there was a mill, and here it got stuck in the weir. Fortunately one of the miller's lads was standing there and he noticed it and pulled it in with a hook, expecting to find it full of treasure—but when he opened it, of course, there was a beautiful little lad, looking up all merry and bright. So he brought him to the folk at the mill, and, since they hadn't got children of their own, they were very pleased, and said, "That's a blessing from God," and they took great care of their foundling and he grew up a fine lad.

Now it so happened that one day, during a thunder-storm, the king came into the mill, and he asked the mill-folk if the tall boy was their son.

"Oh, no," they answered, "he's a foundling. Fourteen years ago he came floating into the weir in a box and one of the lads hooked him out of the water."

So the king saw at once that this was none other than the luck-child that he'd thrown into the water, and he said, "Tell me, good people, can I get this young fellow to carry a letter back to my lady queen? I'll give him a couple of gold pieces as a reward."

"As your Majesty orders," answered the good people, and they called to the lad to get himself ready. Then the king wrote a letter to the queen saying, "As soon as the boy arrives with this letter you must kill him and bury him; and let all be done before I return."

The boy set off with the letter, but lost his way and, come evening, found himself in a big forest. He saw a tiny light shining in the darkness and went towards it and came to a little house. Going in, he found an old woman all alone beside the fire. She was shocked when she saw the lad and she said, "Where are you from and where are you going?"

"I'm from the mill," answered the boy, "and I'm on my way to Her Majesty the Queen with this letter—but I've lost my way in this forest and I'd like to spend the night here."

"You poor young chap," said the woman. "You've landed up in a robbers' house, and when they all get back they'll cut your throat."

"Be that as it may," said the boy. "I'm not frit. Anyway I'm so fagged out I can't go any further," and he stretched himself out on a bench and went to sleep.

Soon after this the robbers came back and asked angrily what sort of a strange fellow this was, lying there.

"Aw," said the old woman, "he's just a poor innocent child, lost his way in the forest. I took him in out of the kindness of me old heart—he's taking a letter to my lady, the queen." So the robbers broke open the letter, read it, and saw there, in black and white, that the boy was to be killed as soon as he arrived. Well, the robbers may have been hard-hearted, but this moved them to pity and their leader tore up the letter and wrote another, saying that as soon as the boy arrived he was to be married to the king's daughter. Then they left him sleeping there on the bench till next morning and, when he'd woken up, they gave him the letter and put him on the right road.

As for the queen, though, once she'd got the letter and read what was in it, she ordered a splendid wedding feast, and the princess was married to the luck-child. And since the young fellow was both handsome and kind she found living with him to be altogether very enjoyable.

After a bit, though, the king came back to his palace and discovered that the prophecy had been fulfilled and his daughter married to the luck-child. "How's this come about?" said he. "I gave quite different orders in my letter." Then the queen reached over his letter and said he could see for himself what was there, and the king read it and saw well enough that it had been swapped with another. So he asked the young man what had happened to the letter he'd entrusted to him and why he'd delivered a different one.

"No idea," he answered, "it must have been changed over in the night, while I was asleep in the forest."

Then the king was furiously angry. "It's not going to be as easy as that for you," he shouted. "Whoever wants to have my daughter must fetch me three golden hairs from the head of the Devil in Hell. You bring me these and then you may keep my daughter."

By this the king hoped to be rid of the lad for good, but the luck-child answered, "I'll fetch you your golden hairs. I'm not afraid of any old devil." And he said good-bye and set out on his travels.

His way led him to a big town where the gate-keeper cross-questioned him about his trade and what sort of things he knew.

"I know everything," answered the luck-child.

"All right then," said the gate-keeper, "you can do us a kindness. You can tell us why our parish-pump that used to flow with wine is all dried up and doesn't even give us water."

"Very well," said the boy, "I'll tell you that, but you must wait for me to come back again."

Then he went along a bit further and came to another town, whose gate-keeper also asked him what his trade was and what he knew. "I know everything," answered the luck-child. "All right then, you can do us a kindness, and tell us why it is that a tree in our town that used to grow golden apples doesn't even put out leaves any more."

"Very well," said the boy, "I'll tell you that, but you must wait for me to come back again."

Then he went along a bit further and came to a huge river that he had to get across. The ferry-man asked him what his trade was and what he knew. "I know everything," answered the luck-child.

"All right then, you can do me a kindness," said the ferry-man, "you can tell me why I must be always poling across here, backwards and forwards, and never get free."

"Very well," said the boy, "I'll tell you that, but you must wait for me to come back again."

Once he was across the water he found himself at the gates of Hell. It was all black and sooty in there and the Devil wasn't at home, but his grandmother was sitting there in a big armchair.

"What d'you want?" says she to him—but she didn't look too frightful.

"What I really want," says he in reply, "is three golden hairs out of the Devil's head—otherwise I'm not to be allowed to keep my wife."

"That's asking a lot," says she. "If the Devil comes home and finds you then he'll fit you up in a hempen collar—but I'm sorry for you. I'll see if I can help." So she changed him into an ant and said, "Crawl into the folds of my gown. You'll be safe there.''

''All right,'' says he, ''that's very kind of you, but there's three things I'd still like to know: why a parish-pump that used to give wine has now dried up and doesn't even give water; why a tree that once grew golden apples doesn't even put out leaves any more; and why a ferry-man must always be poling backwards and forwards and never get free.''

''Them's hard questions,'' says she, ''but just you stay still and quiet and pay heed to what the Devil says when I pull out his three golden hairs.''

As evening fell the Devil came home. As soon as he got in he noticed that the air wasn't wholesome.

''I smell the smell of human flesh,'' said he, ''all's not right here.'' And he poked about in all the corners, looking, but he couldn't find anything.

His grandmother berated him, ''Here have I just swept up,'' she said, ''everything put to rights, and now you come and tip it all upside-down again! You've always got human flesh up your nose! Just you sit down and have your supper!''

When he'd eaten and drunk he was tired so he laid his head in his grandmother's lap and said she should pick a few lice out of his hair. That didn't last long, though, because soon he was fast asleep, snuffling and snoring. Then the old woman got hold of a golden hair, pulled it out and laid it down beside her.

''Youtch!'' yelled the Devil, ''what d'you think you're doing?''

''Ooh, I've had a peculiar dream,'' answered his grandmother, ''and I grabbed you by the hair.''

''What did you dream then?'' asked the Devil.

''I dreamt there was a parish-pump which once gave wine, dried up, and won't even give water now. What's the cause of that?''

''Heh! if they did but know,'' answered the Devil, ''there's a toad under a stone in the pump. If they kill it then the wine'll flow again.''

The grandmother went back to the lice until he was asleep again, and snoring so loud the windows rattled. Then she pulled out the second hair.

''Hoo! what're y'doing'' shouted the Devil angrily.

Seeking a gold hair from the Devil

"Aw don't take on," she answered. "I did it while I was dreaming."

"Well, what have you dreamed this time?" he asked her.

"In a kingdom I dreamt there was a fruit tree which used to grow golden apples, but now won't put out so much as leaves. What's likely to be the cause of that?"

"Heh. if they did but know!" answered the Devil. "There's a mouse gnawing at the root, if they kill him then it'll grow its golden apples again, but if he gnaws much longer the whole tree'll wither. But let me alone with all your dreaming, if you disturb my slumbers once more I'll box your ears."

The grandmother calmed him down and went back to the lice until he was asleep again and snoring. Then she seized the third golden hair and pulled it out. The Devil leapt up in the air, yelled, and was all ready to come to a fine old reckoning, but she quieted him down yet again and said, "What can you do about bad dreams!"

"What've you dreamed this time then?" he asked, wanting to know in spite of himself.

"I dreamed about a ferry-man, fed up with having to pole hither and yon and never get free. What's the cause of that?"

"Heh, the chucklehead," answered the Devil, "when someone comes along that wants to get across, he must put the pole into his hand, then the other'll have to do the ferrying and he can go free." So now that the grandmother had pulled out the three golden hairs and got answers to the three questions she left the old dragon in peace and he went on sleeping till break of day.

When the Devil had gone away again, the old woman picked the ant out of the fold in her robe and gave the luck-child his human form again. "There are your three golden hairs," she said, "and you must have heard what the Devil said about your three questions."

"Yes," he answered, "I heard it all and I'll remember it all."

"Then that's been a help," she said, "so now you can be on your way."

He thanked the old woman for getting him out of his troubles, turned his back on Hell, and was glad that everything was working out so happily. When he came to the ferry-man he had to give him the promised answer.

"Take me across first," said the luck-child, "then I'll tell you how to get free." And when he'd got to the further shore he gave him the Devil's advice: "When somebody else comes along who wants to get across, just put the pole into his hand."

Then he went on his way till he came to the town with the barren tree, where the watchman also wanted his answer. So he told him what he'd heard from the Devil: "Kill the mouse gnawing the root, and it'll give golden apples again," and the watchman thanked him and gave him as a reward two asses laden with gold to follow him home.

Then finally he came to the town with the dried-up pump, and he told the watchman what the Devil had said: "There's a toad sitting in the pump under a stone—seek him out and kill him and your wine will start flowing again." And the watchman thanked him and likewise gave him a couple of asses laden with gold.

Eventually the luck-child got back home to his wife, who was overjoyed to see him again and to hear how well he'd succeeded with everything. He brought to the king what he'd demanded—the Devil's three golden hairs—and when the king saw the four asses with all that gold he was delighted and said, "Now you've met the bargain you can keep my daughter. But tell me, my dearest son-in-law, where did you come by all that gold? This is real treasure!"

"Oh—I crossed a river," he answered, " and took it away with me. It's lying around there on the banks instead of sand."

"Well, can I fetch some too?" asked the king, lusting after the gold.

"Yes, as much as you want—there's a ferry-man by the river. Let him take you over, then you can fill your sacks on the other side."

The greedy king set off as quick as he could, and when he came to the river he beckoned to the ferry-man to take him over. The ferry-man came and bade him get in, and when they got to the farther shore he handed him the pole and leapt away—so from then on the king had to do the ferrying as a punishment for his sins.

"And is he still ferrying?"
"What else? Nobody's taken his pole."

The Story of the Juniper Tree

Well—it were all a long time back—as good as two thousand year—and there was this rich man that had a lovely, god-fearing young wife. And the two of them loved each other from the bottom of their hearts—but they had no children. Much good wishing—much good the woman praying and carrying on day and night—they got none, and they got none.

Now at the front of their house there was a courtyard with a juniper tree in it—and one winter's day the woman was standing there underneath it peeling herself an apple; and as she peeled the apple she cut herself in the finger so that the blood dripped down on the snow. "Aah!" said the woman, fetching up a great sigh, and looking at the blood all sorrowful. "Aah—that I might have a child as red as that blood and as white as that snow." And no sooner had she said that than she felt real glad—just as if it were all going to happen.

So she went back in the house, and after a month had passed the snow melted—two months and it were all greening—three months and the flowers came up out the ground—four months and all the trees blossomed in the woods, and the green branches grew in great tangles. The little birds sang there, filling all the woods with their singing, and the blossom dropped from the trees. Then the fifth month was by, and she stood under the juniper tree, that smelt so lovely, and her heart leapt and she fell to her knees and hugged herself for joy. And when the sixth month was past, the fruit grew fat and heavy and she came over all quiet; and the seventh month she grabbed after the juniper-berries and ate them so greedily that she turned sad and ill. Then the eighth month went by and she called her man over and wept and said, "If I die, you must bury me under the juniper tree." Then she was comforted and full of happiness till the ninth month was gone, and then she had a child—as white as snow and as red as blood. And when she saw that, she was so overcome with joy that she died.

Then her man buried her under the juniper tree and began to weep bitter tears. After a bit, though, he felt easier, and after he'd cried for a while longer he pulled himself together and, after a bit more, he got married again.

Along with this second wife he got a daughter—but the child of his first wife was a little son, and was as red as blood and as white as snow. Now whenever the woman looked at her daughter, she loved her, but whenever she turned to the little lad it would cut her to the heart—it seemed to her that all the time he was standing in her way, and she kept thinking how she might get all the riches for her daughter, and the Devil worked on her so that she was real horrid to the little lad, shoving him around from one corner to another, biffing him here, cuffing him there, so that the poor child lived in fear. When he came out of school there was never a quiet spot for him to settle in.

One day the woman had gone up to her room and her little daughter came up too and said, "Mother, give us an apple."

"All right, my dear," said the woman, and gave her a beautiful apple out of the chest (and this chest had a great heavy lid with a great sharp iron hasp to it).

"Mother," said the little daughter, "shan't brother have one too?"

That vexed the woman, but she said, "All right, when he gets back from school." And when she saw through the window that he was on his way it was just as if the Devil had got into her and she snatched the apple off her daughter and said, "You'll not have that before your brother," and she flung the apple into the chest and shut the lid on it.

Then the little boy came in the door and the Devil made her say to him all friendly, "Now then, my lad, would you like an apple?" and she looked at him wicked awful.

"Why, mother," said the little boy, "what are you looking all nasty like that for? Yes—give me an apple!"

Then it came over her that she must tempt him more. "Come with me," she said, and opened up the lid. "Take yourself an apple out of there." And as the little boy ducked his head in—like that—the Devil prompted her, and, bang! she slammed the lid to so that his head flew off and fell among the red apples. Then she was overcome with fear and thought to herself, "How can I get out of this?" and she went up to her room, to her chest-of-drawers, and pulled a white cloth out of the top drawer. Then she set the head back on its neck and tied the cloth round like a scarf, so that you couldn't see anything, and she sat the boy down on a chair by the door and put the apple into his hand.

Then little Malinka came through to her mother in the kitchen, who was standing by the fire and had a pot of hot water in front of her, stirring and stirring it. "Mother," said little Malinka, "brother's sitting here by the door, looking all white, and he's got an apple in his hands. I've told him he should give me the apple, but he won't say anything. He's making me all cross."

"Go on back to him," said the mother, "and if he still won't say anything to you give him a box on the ears."

So little Malinka went back and said, "Brother, give me the apple." But he stayed there quiet, so she gave him a box on the ears, and down fell his head. She was terrified at that and set up a crying and a roaring and ran to her mother and said. "Oh, mother, I've knocked my brother's head off," and she wept and wept and wouldn't be comforted.

"Oh, little Malinka," said the mother, "what've you done? But wait on—quiet—so's no one'll notice—there's no changing things now; we'll cook him in the stew." So the mother took the little lad and chopped him up in pieces, threw him in the pot and cooked him in the stew. As for little

Malinka, though, she stood there crying and crying, and the tears all fell into the pot—so they had no call to use any salt.

When the father got home he sat himself down at the table and said, "Well—where's my boy then?" The mother heaved up a huge great tureen of black stew, and little Malinka cried and couldn't stop crying. Then the father said again, "Well—where's my boy then?"

"Aw," said the mother, "he's gone traipsing off to see his old mother's uncle—he'll be staying there for a while."

"What the heck's he doing there—and never said good-bye to me?"

"Oh, he was so much after going that he asked me if he could stay over there six weeks. You can be sure they'll take good care of him."

"Aw," said the man, "I'm real sorry about that. It's not right, y'know. He should have said good-bye to me." With that he got on with his supper, and said, "Malinka, what are you crying for? Brother'll be back again soon." Then later: "By gosh, woman, that's a tasty bit of stew— give us some more." And the more he ate the more he had to have, and he said, "Come on, give us some more—you'll none of you have any of this—it's all for me." And he ate and he ate, and he threw the bones down under the table till he'd finished the lot.

As for little Malinka, though, she went to her cupboard and out from the darkest shelf she brought her best silken shawl, and she fetched out all the little joints and bones from under the table and tied them up in the silken shawl and carried them outside, weeping bloody tears. Then she laid them down under the juniper tree in the green grass, and when she'd set them all out she suddenly felt easy and stopped her crying. Then the juniper tree began to move, and its branches lifted themselves each from the other and came together again, just like someone rejoicing and clapping his hands. At the same time a mist rose from the tree, and right inside the mist a burning—like fire—and out of the fire there flew a beautiful bird, singing so it was wonderful to hear, and he flew off high into the sky, and when he was gone the juniper tree was just as it had always been and the shawl and the bones were gone too. But little Malinka was light-hearted and happy just as though her brother was still alive—and she went back in the house, all cheerful, sat down at the table and ate up her supper.

Now the bird had flown away to a goldsmith's house and begun to
sing:
>   "My mother, she slew me,
>   My father, he ate me,
>   My sister Malinka,
>   She gathers up my bones;
>   She ties them in a silken shawl
>   And lays them under the juniper tree.
>   Kiwhitt, kiwhitt,
>   What a beautiful bird am I."

The goldsmith was sitting in his workshop fashioning a golden chain.
He heard the bird sitting up on his roof, singing, and he thought he had
heard nothing so beautiful. So he stood up, and as he went over the door-
sill he lost one of his slippers. But he set off away up the middle of the
street, one shoe off and one shoe on, with his apron round his middle and
in one hand the golden chain and in the other his pincers—and the sun
shone over the street. So he stood right there and looked at the bird.

"Bird," says he, "that's beautiful singing! Sing me that piece again."

"Nay," says the bird, "I don't sing twice for nothing. Give me that
golden chain and I'll sing it through again."

"There," says the goldsmith, "you can have the golden chain, now
sing me that again." So the bird flew down, took the golden chain in his
right claw, sat down in front of the goldsmith and sang:
>   "My mother, she slew me,
>   My father, he ate me,
>   My sister Malinka,
>   She gathers up my bones;
>   She ties them in a silken shawl
>   And lays them under the juniper tree.
>   Kiwhitt, kiwhitt,
>   What a beautiful bird am I."

Then the bird flew off to a cobbler, and sat up on his roof and sang:
>   "My mother, she slew me,
>   My father, he ate me,
>   My sister Malinka,

She gathers up my bones;
She ties them in a silken shawl
And lays them under the juniper tree.
Kiwhitt, kiwhitt,
What a beautiful bird am I."

The cobbler heard him and leapt out of doors in his shirt-sleeves and looked up at his roof (but he had to hold his hand over his eyes so that the sun shouldn't dazzle him). "Bird," says he, "that's beautiful singing"—and he called indoors, "Hey, missus, come out here a minute! There's a bird here—just look at that bird—he don't half sing well." And he called his daughter and children and apprentices, boys and girls, and they all came up the street and looked at the bird—what a beauty he was, with all his red and green feathers, and those round his neck like pure gold, and his eyes shining in his head like stars.

"Bird," says the cobbler, "just sing that piece again."

"Nay," says the bird, "I don't sing twice for nothing. You'll have to give me something."

"Woman," says the man, "get up to the attic—up there, on the top shelf, there's a pair of red shoes—bring 'em down here." So the woman went in and fetched the shoes. "There, bird," says the man, "now sing me that piece again." So the bird came and took the shoes in his left claw and flew back up to the roof and sang:

"My mother, she slew me,
My father, he ate me,
My sister Malinka,
She gathers up my bones;
She ties them in a silken shawl
And lays them under the juniper tree.
Kiwhitt, kiwhitt,
What a beautiful bird am I."

And when he'd done singing he flew off, the chain in his right claw and the shoes in his left, and he flew far off to a mill and the mill went "clipper, clapper, clipper, clapper, clipper, clapper," and in the mill there were twenty miller-lads sitting cutting a stone and chipping away at it "hick, hack, hick, hack, hick, hack," while the mill went "clipper,

clapper, clipper, clapper, clipper, clapper". Then the bird went up and
sat in a linden tree that stood in front of the mill, and he sang:
"My mother, she slew me,"
and one stopped,
"My father, he ate me,"
and two more stopped and listened
"My sister Malinka"
and four more stopped,
"She gathers up my bones;
She ties them in a silken shawl"
and now only eight men were chipping,
"And lays them under"
now only five men
"the juniper tree."
now only one man
"Kiwhitt, kiwhitt,
What a beautiful bird am I."
and the last man stopped too, but all he heard was the last bit. "Bird,"
says he, "that's beautiful singing! Let me listen too, sing it all again."
"Nay," says the bird, "I don't sing twice for nothing. If you'll give me
that mill-stone then I'll sing it again."
"All right," says he, "if it just belonged to me you should have it."
"All right," said the others, "if he'll sing again he shall have it." So the
bird came down and the miller-lads set to—all twenty of 'em—with a
beam and levered up the stone "hey, oop, hey, oop, hey, oop" and the
bird poked his neck through the hole in the stone, putting it on like a
collar, and flew up into the tree again and sang:
"My mother, she slew me,
My father, he ate me,
My sister Malinka,
She gathers up my bones;
She ties them in a silken shawl
And lays them under the juniper tree.
Kiwhitt, kiwhitt,
What a beautiful bird am I."

And when he'd done singing he spread out his wings, with the chain in his right claw, the shoes in his left claw and the mill-stone round his neck, and he flew away back to his father's house.

The father, the mother and little Malinka were in the room, sitting round the table, and the father was saying, "By Gosh, I feel in a right good mood—not a care in the world!"

"Well I don't," said the mother. "I've got forebodings like there was going to be an almighty thunderstorm." But little Malinka sat there, crying and crying, till the bird flew by—and as he settled himself on the roof the father said, "I'm that cheerful and the sun's shining so bright, I feel like I was going to meet up with old friends again."

"Never," said the woman, "I'm that fearful my teeth are chattering and I feel like I've got fire running down my veins." And she started to tear open all the front of her dress, but little Malinka sat in a corner and cried (she had her plate there in front of her eyes, crying over it till it was all sticky). Then the bird sat in the juniper tree and sang:

"My mother, she slew me"
and the mother covered her ears and shut her eyes and wouldn't look or listen, but there was rumbling in her ears like the wildest storm and her eyes burned and flashed like lightning.

"My father, he ate me"
"Why, mother," says the man, "there's a lovely bird, singing so beautifully, and the sun shining so warm and everything smelling like cinnamon."

"My sister Malinka"
and little Malinka leant her head on her knee and almost wept her eyes out, but the man said, "I'm going out there; I must see that bird close to."

"Aw, don't go," said the woman, "the whole house seems to be shaking and going up in flames." But the man went out and looked at the bird.

"She gathers up my bones;
She ties them in a silken shawl
And lays them under the juniper tree.
Kiwhitt, kiwhitt,
What a beautiful bird am I."

185

With that the bird let fall the golden chain and it fell on the man, right round his neck and it fitted him perfectly. Then he went back in and said, "Look! how's that for a marvellous bird—it's given me such a beautiful golden chain, and looks so beautiful as well." But the woman was frightened out of her wits, fell down on the floor and her cap fell off her head. Then the bird sang again:

"My mother, she slew me"

"Aah—that I were a thousand fathoms in the ground so as not to hear it!"

"My father, he ate me"

And the woman fell down as though dead.

"My sister Malinka"

"Oh!" said Malinka "I'll go out there too and see if the bird'll give me something." And she went out:

"She gathers up my bones;
    She ties them in a silken shawl"

Then he threw down the shoes to her:

"And lays them under the juniper tree.
    Kiwhitt, kiwhitt,
    What a beautiful bird am I."

Then Malinka turned all glad and merry. She put on the new red shoes and danced and jumped about, back indoors. "Hey," she said, "I was so sad when I went out there and now everything's so bonny—that's a wonderful bird—look! he's given me a pair of red shoes."

"Nay," said the woman, and jumped up, and her hair stood on end like flames of fire, "I reckon the world's falling to pieces—I'm off out there too to see if I feel better." And as she went out the door—bam!—the bird dropped the mill-stone on her head and she was squashed flat.

The father and little Malinka heard that and went out. Smoke and flames and fire were leaping up from the spot and as it scattered away, there was little brother standing there. And he took his father and little Malinka by the hand and they were all three so happy they went back in the house together, sat down at the table, and finished their supper.

The Golden Key

Once upon a time, in the depths of winter, with the snow lying in great drifts, a poor boy was sent out to bring in wood on a sledge. When he'd found all he wanted, and piled it all up, he decided—because he was so freezing cold—that he wouldn't go home just yet but would make a fire and warm himself up a bit. So he raked away the snow, and just as he was clearing a patch of earth he found a tiny golden key. "Aha," said he to himself, "where there's a key, there must be a lock," and he burrowed in the ground and discovered an iron casket. "If only the key fits!" he thought, "there's surely precious things in this box." He peered about but there didn't seem to be a key-hole—then, at last, he found one, but so small that you could hardly see it. He tried it, and the key fitted perfectly. Then he turned it once . . .

. . . and now we must wait till it's completely unlocked, with the lid open, so that we can see what wonderful things are really there, lying in the casket.

187

Afterword

In telling or reading stories to children during the last few years I have become increasingly uneasy about the treatment accorded to the Brothers Grimm by their English translators. All too often their *Märchen* ("strange little tales"—the word itself is impossible to cope with) have been mistranslated or bowdlerised or, worst of all, set down in versions which may be accurate as to the letter but which miss the spirit of the tales. It seems to me that the translator should never forget that his original stemmed not from a scholar's study but from a storyteller talking to his listeners.

In undertaking this new translation, therefore, I have tried to bring into my English texts something of the unselfconscious directness and the colloquial ease which are characteristic of the *Märchen* at their best. Where the original is very close to an oral mode—especially in dialect stories—I have tried to retain this in English; and where there are more 'literary' effects and embellishments I have still tried to give a fluency to the story which will make it pleasant to read aloud. From time to time, therefore, the translation of words or phrases may have been modified— but this has only been done at points where I consider that the modification makes the language of the story natural for the English teller in the same way that it is natural for the German one.

It should also be said that the stories collected by the Brothers Grimm exist in a number of forms. There are manuscripts, printed versions as first published (in two volumes in Berlin, 1812 and 1815), and printed versions as later prepared under the supervision of the Brothers—but usually Wilhelm—where modifications and extensions may have occurred to smooth out the original roughnesses of the stories. The generally accepted 'canon' of the tales is that of just such a late reworking of the original texts. It contains 201 stories (numbered 1–200, with two stories numbered 151) and ten 'Children's Legends' as a supplement.

The present translation is largely based on texts which had reached this final form, the ninth edition of the 'Grosse Ausgabe' (1870) being used as a copy-text. In some instances, however, comparison with previous versions (especially those printed in Heinz Rölleke's *Die älteste Märchensammlung der Brüder Grimm*, Geneva, 1975) has given rise to a change in policy, and this is indicated in the following notes.

Perhaps it should also be said that the choice of stories for translation has been governed by the whim of the translator—modified at times by suggestions from publisher and illustrator—and that the arrangement of the book has been consciously devised. It was hoped that the sequence of stories would have a naturalness about it that would make it comfortable for readers to work through, if they wished, from one end to the other. This has also enabled the illustrator, on some occasions, to apply a unifying idea to a group of pictures.

The following notes mention any special points that seem relevant to the present translation. They also give the German titles of the stories and the numbers that are usually attached to them.

Notes

1. 'A Story to Begin With' (Das Dietmarsische Lügenmärchen no. 159)—that is to say 'Dietmar's Tale of Lies'.

2. Little Louse and Little Flea (Läuschen und Flöhchen no. 30)—a translation probably influenced by many happy readings of Joseph Jacobs's 'Titty Mouse and Tatty Mouse' in *English Fairy Tales*, London, 1890.

3. Whisp of Straw, Lump of Coal, and Little Broad Bean (Strohhalm, Kohle und Bohne no. 18).

4. The Wolf and the Seven Little Kids (Der Wolf und die sieben jungen Geislein no. 5)— translated from the manuscript version given in Rölleke, but with reference to later editions.

5. The Bremen Town Musicians (Die Bremer Stadtmusikanten no. 27). The cock's remark about 'calling up good weather for a Saturday' replaces a more involved and localised explanation about this being 'the day when Our Lady hangs the Christ Child's nightshirts out to dry'. No comprehensible English translation seemed possible for this customary saying. The original storyteller's rounding-off line for this story also seemed a bit gnomic and has been replaced by an English form.

6. The Seven Ravens (Die sieben Raben no. 25).

7. Rapunzel (Rapunzel no. 12). The translation follows Wilhelm Grimm's later version of the story. In the first edition (1812) the witch discovers that Rapunzel is seeing the Prince because Rapunzel gets pregnant—hence the twins.

8. Briar-Rose; or the Sleeping Beauty (Dornröschen no. 50)—

translated in the main from the first printing of 1812, with some small details added from the later, longer version.

9. Jorinde and Joringel (Jorinde und Joringel no. 69).

10. Little Snow-White (Sneewittchen no. 53).

11. Little Brother and Little Sister (Brüderchen und Schwesterchen no. 11).

12. The Frog King; or Iron Henry (Der Froschkönig; oder der eiserne Heinrich no. 1).

13. Fitcher's Bird (Fitchers Vogel no. 46)—a hauntingly weird version of the Bluebeard story. Like most of the little rhymes that appear in the Grimm stories, those here are impossible to translate adequately. For a superior attempt see that by Lore Segal in Volume 1 of *The Juniper Tree*, New York 1973, London 1974.

14. The Merry Tale of the Clever Little Tailor (Vom klugen Schneiderlein no. 114). This translation was originally made for a new edition of Andrew Lang's *Green Fairy Book*, London 1978, and is used here by kind permission of Kestrel Books.

15. The Sad Tale of Clever Elsie (Die kluge Else no. 34). The abrupt ending to this tale is not greatly improved upon in the similar, but more farcical, ending to 'Der Frieder und das Catherlieschen', which is well-known in England as 'Frederick and Kate-Elizabeth'. Neither tale manages the treatment of the stupid betrothed so well as the neater, more good-humoured 'Three Sillies' in Jacobs's *English Fairy Tales*, London 1890.

16. Lazy 'Arry, Sunny Jim and Skinny Lizzie. Taking a hint from references present in the Grimms' text, these three tales are combined from 'Der faule Heinz' no. 64, 'Der kluge Knecht' no. 162, and 'Die hagere Liese' no. 168.

17. The Moon (Der Mond no. 175).

18. Godfather Death (Der Gevatter Tod no. 44).

19. The Fisherman and his Wife (Von dem Fischer un syner Fru no. 19). As with 'The Clever Little Tailor'—no. 14 above—this was originally translated for a new edition of Andrew Lang's *Green Fairy Book*, and the tale is included by kind permission of Kestrel Books. The North Country dialect which is suggested is intended to correspond with

the North German dialect of the Grimms' tale.

20. King Throstlebeard (König Drosselbart no. 52). Variant English names for the king are 'Grisly-beard' and 'Thrushbeard'. The present title has been chosen as corresponding more closely with the sound of the German.

21. The Twelve Dancing Princesses; or The Shoes that were Danced to Pieces (Die zertanzten Schuhe no. 133).

22. Six Men Go Far Together in the Wide World (Sechse kommen durch die ganze Welt no. 71).

23. The Blue Light (Das blaue Licht no. 116).

24. Hansel and Gretel (Hänsel und Grethel no. 15).

25. Rumpelstiltskin (Rumpelstilzchen no. 55).

26. Hans My Hedgehog (Hans mein Igel no. 108). No attempt has been made at a direct translation of the final couplet 'Mein Märchen ist aus / Und geht vor Gustchen sein Haus'.

27. The Goose-girl (Die Gänsemagd no. 89). The repeated, plaintive first couplet in this story is materially that used by Andrew Lang in the translation that appeared in *The Blue Fairy Book*, London 1889.

28. Boots of Buffalo Leather (Der Stiefel von Büffelleder no. 199).

29. The Three Golden Hairs of the Devil (Der Teufel mit den drei goldenen Haaren no. 29). The *Oxford English Dictionary* says of the word 'caul' that this is part of the foetal membrane 'sometimes enveloping the head of the child at birth, superstitiously regarded as of good omen, and supposed to be a preservative against drowning'.

30. The Juniper Tree (Von dem Machandelboom no. 47).

31. The Golden Key (Der goldene Schlüssel no. 200).